Robert Stawell Ball

Time and Tide

A Romance of the Moon

Robert Stawell Ball

Time and Tide
A Romance of the Moon

ISBN/EAN: 9783744673983

Printed in Europe, USA, Canada, Australia, Japan

Cover: Foto ©Thomas Meinert / pixelio.de

More available books at **www.hansebooks.com**

VIEW OF THE MOON TWO DAYS AFTER FIRST QUARTER.
From a photograph by Mr. LEWIS M. RUTHERFORD.

Frontispiece.

THE ROMANCE OF SCIENCE.

TIME AND TIDE,

A Romance of the Moon.

BEING TWO LECTURES DELIVERED
IN THE THEATRE OF THE LONDON INSTITUTION,
ON THE AFTERNOONS OF NOVEMBER 19 AND 26, 1888.

BY

SIR ROBERT S. BALL, LL.D., F.R.S.,

AUTHOR OF "STARLAND";
LOWNDEAN PROFESSOR OF ASTRONOMY AND GEOMETRY IN THE UNIVERSITY
OF CAMBRIDGE.

SECOND EDITION, REVISED.

PUBLISHED UNDER THE DIRECTION OF THE COMMITTEE OF
GENERAL LITERATURE AND EDUCATION APPOINTED
BY THE SOCIETY FOR PROMOTING CHRISTIAN
KNOWLEDGE,

LONDON:
SOCIETY FOR PROMOTING CHRISTIAN KNOWLEDGE.
NEW YORK: E. & J. B. YOUNG & CO.
1892.

TO

The Members of the London Institution

I DEDICATE

THIS LITTLE BOOK.

PREFACE.

HAVING been honoured once again with a request that I should lecture before the London Institution, I chose for my subject the Theory of Tidal Evolution. The kind reception which these lectures received has led to their publication in the present volume. I have taken the opportunity to supplement the lectures as actually delivered by the insertion of some additional matter. I am indebted to my friends Mr. Close and Mr. Rambaut for their kindness in reading the proofs.

ROBERT S. BALL.

Observatory, CO. DUBLIN,
  April 26, 1889.

PREFACE TO THE SECOND EDITION.

In the present Edition I have taken the opportunity of making sundry verbal corrections. I may also remark that the reader is presumed to be acquainted with such ordinary astronomical facts as would be contained in a book of the scope of my little volume *Starland*.

ROBERT S. BALL.

May 1st, 1892.

TIME AND TIDE.

LECTURE I.

IT is my privilege to address you this afternoon on a subject in which science and poetry are blended in a happy conjunction. If there be a peculiar fascination about the earlier chapters of any branch of history, how great must be the interest which attaches to that most primeval of all terrestrial histories which relates to the actual beginnings of this globe on which we stand.

In our efforts to grope into the dim recesses of this awful past, we want the aid of some steadfast light which shall illumine the dark places without the treachery of the will-o'-the-wisp. In the absence of that steadfast light, vague conjectures as to the beginning of things could never be entitled to any more respect than was due to mere matters of speculation.

Of late, however, the required light has been to some considerable extent forthcoming, and the attempt has been made, with no little success, to elucidate a most interesting and wonderful chapter of an exceedingly remote history. To chronicle this history is the object of the present lectures before this Institution.

First, let us be fully aware of the extraordinary remoteness of that period of which our history treats. To attempt to define that period chronologically would be utterly futile. When we have stated that it is more ancient than almost any other period which we can discuss, we have expressed all that we are really entitled to say. Yet this conveys not a little. It directs us to look back through all the ages of modern human history, through the great days of ancient Greece and Rome, back through the times when Egypt and Assyria were names of renown, through the days when Nineveh and Babylon were mighty and populous cities in the zenith of their glory. Back earlier still to those more ancient nations of which

we know hardly anything, and still earlier to
the prehistoric man, of whom we know less ; back,
finally, to the days when man first trod on this
planet, untold ages ago. Here is indeed a por-
tentous retrospect from most points of view, but
it is only the commencement of that which our
subject suggests.

For man is but the final product of the long
anterior ages during which the development of life
seems to have undergone an exceedingly gradual
elevation.   Our retrospect now takes its way along
the vistas opened up by the geologists. We look
through the protracted tertiary ages, when mighty
animals, now generally extinct, roamed over the
continents. Back still earlier through those wondrous secondary periods, where swamps or oceans
often covered what is now dry land, and where
mighty reptiles of uncouth forms stalked and
crawled and swam through the old world and the
new. Back still earlier through those vitally significant ages when the sunbeams were being
garnered and laid aside for man's use in the great
forests, which were afterwards preserved by being
transformed into seams of coal. Back still earlier

through endless thousands of years, when lustrous
fishes abounded in the oceans ; back again to those
periods characterized by the lower types of life ;
and still earlier to that incredibly remote epoch
when life itself began to dawn on our awakening
globe. Even here the epoch of our present history
can hardly be said to have been reached. We
have to look through a long succession of ages
still antecedent. The geologist, who has hitherto
guided our view, cannot render us much further
assistance ; but the physicist is at hand—he teaches
us that the warm globe on which life is beginning
has passed in its previous stages through every
phase of warmth, of fervour, of glowing heat, of
incandescence, and of actual fusion ; and thus at
last our retrospect reaches that particular period
of our earth's past history which is specially
illustrated by the modern doctrine of Time and
Tide.

The present is the clue to the past. It is the
steady application of this principle which has led
to such epoch-making labours as those by which
Lyell investigated the origin of the earth's crust,
Darwin the origin of species, Max Müller the origin

of language. In our present subject the course
is plain. Study exactly what is going on at
present, and then have the courage to apply consistently and rigorously what we have learned
from the present to the interpretation of the
past.

Thus we begin with the ripple of the tide on the
sea-beach which we see to-day. The ebb and the
flow of the tide are the present manifestations of
an agent which has been constantly at work. Let
that present teach us what tides must have done in
the indefinite past.

It has been known from the very earliest times
that the moon and the tides were connected
together—connected, I say, for a great advance
had to be made in human knowledge before it
would have been possible to understand the true
relation between the tides and the moon. Indeed,
that relation is so far from being of an obvious
character, that I think I have read of a race who
felt some doubt as to whether the moon was the
cause of the tides, or the tides the cause of the
moon. I should, however, say that the moon is
not the sole agent engaged in producing this

periodic movement of our waters. The sun also
arouses a tide, but the solar tide is so small in
comparison with that produced by the moon, that
for our present purpose we may leave it out of
consideration. We must, however, refer to the
solar tide at a later period of our discourses, for
it will be found to have played a splendid part
at the initial stage of the Earth-Moon History,
while in the remote future it will again rise into
prominence.

It will be well to set forth a few preliminary
figures which shall explain how it comes to pass
that the efficiency of the sun as a tide-producing
agent is so greatly inferior to that of the moon.
Indeed, considering that the sun has a mass so
stupendous, that it controls the entire planetary
system, it seems strange that a body so insignificant
as the moon can raise a bigger tide on the ocean
than can the sun, of which the mass is 26,000,000
times as great as that of our satellite ?

This apparent paradox will disappear when we
enunciate the law according to which the efficiency
of a tide-producing agent is to be estimated. This
law is somewhat different from the familiar form in

which the law of gravitation is expressed. The gravitation between two distant masses is to be measured by multiplying these masses together, and dividing the product by the *square* of the distance. The law for expressing the efficiency of a tide-producing agent varies not according to the inverse square, but according to the inverse *cube* of the distance. This difference in the expression of the law will suffice to account for the superiority of the moon as a tide-producer over the sun. The moon's distance on an average is about one 386th part of that of the sun, and thus it is easy to show that so far as the mere attraction of gravitation is concerned, the efficiency of the sun's force on the earth is about one hundred and seventy-five times as great as the force with which the moon attracts the earth. That is of course calculated under the law of the inverse square. To determine the tidal efficiency we have to divide this by three hundred and eighty-six, and thus we see that the tidal efficiency of the sun is less than half that of the moon.

When the solar tide and the lunar tide are acting in unison, they conspire to produce very high tides and very low tides, or, as we call them, spring tides. On the other hand, when the sun is so placed as to give us a low tide while the moon is producing a high tide, the net result that we actually experience is merely the excess of the lunar tide over the solar tide ; these are what we call neap tides. In fact, by very careful and long-continued observations of the rise and fall of the tides at a particular port, it becomes possible to determine with accuracy the relative ranges of spring tides and neap tides ; and as the spring tides are produced by moon plus sun, while the neap tides are produced by moon minus sun, we obtain a means of actually weighing the relative masses of the sun and moon. This is one of the remarkable facts which can be deduced from a prolonged study of the tides.

The demonstration of the law of the tide-producing force is of a mathematical character, and I do not intend in these lectures to enter into mathematical calculations. There is, however, a simple line of reasoning which, though it falls short of actual demonstration, may yet suffice to give a plausible reason for the law.

The tides owe their origin to the circumstance
that the tide-producing agent operates more power-
fully on those parts of the tide-exhibiting body
which are near to it, than on the more distant portions of the same. The nearer the two bodies are
together, the larger will be the relative differences
in the distances of its various parts from the tide-
producing body ; and on this account the leverage,
so to speak, of the action by which the tides are
produced is increased. For instance, if the two
bodies were brought within half their original distance of each other, the relative size of each body,
as viewed from the other, will be doubled ; and
what we have called the leverage of the tide-producing ability will be increased twofold. The
gravitation also between the two bodies is increased fourfold when the distance is halved, and
consequently, the tide-producing ability is doubled
for one reason, and increased fourfold again by
another ; hence, the tides will be increased eight-
fold when the distance is reduced to one half.
Now, as eight is the cube of two, this illustration
may be taken as a verification of the law, that
the efficiency of a body as a tide-producer varies

inversely as the cube of the distance between it
and the body on which the tides are being raised.

For simplicity we may make the assumption
that the whole of the earth is submerged beneath
the ocean, and that the moon revolves in the plane
of the equator. We may also entirely neglect for
the present the tides produced by the sun, and we
shall also make the further assumption that friction is absent. What friction is capable of doing
we must, however, refer to later on. The moon
will act on the ocean and deform it, so that there
will be high tide along one meridian, and high
tide also on the opposite meridian. This is indeed
one of the paradoxes by which students are
frequently puzzled when they begin to learn
about the tides. That the moon should pull the
water up in a heap on one side seems plausible
enough. High tide will of course be there; and the
student might naturally think that the water being
drawn in this way into a heap on one side, there
will of course be low tide on the opposite side of
the earth. A natural assumption, perhaps, but
nevertheless a very wrong one. There are at
every moment two opposite parts of the earth in

a condition of high water; in fact, this will be
obvious if we remember that every day, or, to speak
a little more accurately, in every twenty-four hours
and fifty-one minutes, we have on the average
two high tides at each locality.   Of course this
could not be if the moon raised only one heap
of high water, because, as the moon only appears
to revolve around the earth once a day, or, more
accurately, once in that same average period of
twenty-four hours and fifty-one minutes, it would
be impossible for us to have high tides succeeding
each other as they do in periods a little longer
than twelve hours, if only one heap were carried
round the earth.

The first question then is, as to how these two
opposite heaps of water are placed in respect to
the position of the moon.   The most obvious explanation would seem to be, that the moon should
pull the waters up into a heap directly underneath
it, and that therefore there should be high water
underneath the moon.   As to the other side, the
presence of a high tide there was, on this theory,
to be accounted for by the fact that the moon
pulled the earth away from the waters on the more

B 2

remote side, just as it pulled the waters away from
the more remote earth on the side underneath the
moon. It is, however, certainly not the case that
the high tide is situated in the simple position
that this law would indicate, and which we have
represented in Fig. 1, where the circular body is
the earth, the ocean surrounding which is distorted
by the action of the tides.

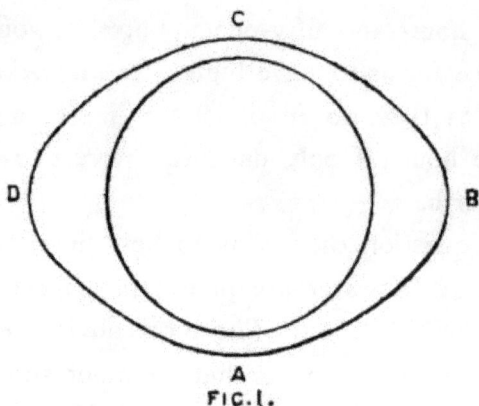

FIG. I.

We have here taken an oval to represent the
shape into which the water is supposed to be
forced or drawn by the tidal action of the tide-
producing body. This may possibly be a correct
representation of what would occur on an ideal

globe entirely covered with a frictionless ocean.
But as our earth is not covered entirely by water,
and as the ocean is very far from being frictionless,
the ideal tide is not the tide that we actually know;
nor is the ideal tide represented by this oval even
an approximation to the actual tides to which
our oceans are subject. Indeed, the oval does not
represent the facts at all, and of this it is only
necessary to adduce a single fact in demonstration.
I take the fundamental issue so often debated, as
to whether in the ocean vibrating with ideal tides
the high water or the low water should be under
the moon. Or to put the matter otherwise; when
we represent the displaced water by an oval, is
the long axis of the oval to be turned to the
moon, as generally supposed, or is it to be directed
at right angles therefrom? If the ideal tides were
in any degree representative of the actual tides, so
fundamental a question as this could be at once
answered by an appeal to the facts of observation.
Even if friction in some degree masked the phenomena, surely one would think that the state of
the actual tides should still enable us to answer
this question.

But a study of the tides at different ports fails to realize this expectation. At some ports, no doubt, the tide is high when the moon is on the meridian. In that case, of course, the high water is under the moon, as apparently ought to be the case invariably, on a superficial view. But, on the other hand, there are ports where there is often low water when the moon is crossing the meridian. Yet other ports might be cited in which every intermediate phase could be observed. If the theory of the tides was to be the simple one so often described, then at every port noon should be the hour of high water on the day of the new moon or of the full moon, because then both tide-exciting bodies are on the meridian at the same time. Even if the friction retarded the great tidal wave uniformly, the high tide on the days of full or change should always occur at fixed hours; but, unfortunately, there is no such delightful theory of the tides as this would imply. At Greenock no doubt there is high water at or about noon on the day of full or change; and if it could be similariy said that on the day of full or change there was high water everywhere at local noon, then

the equilibrium theory of the tides, as it is called,
would be beautifully simple. But this is not the
case. Even around our own coasts the discrepancies are such as to utterly discredit the theory
as offering any practical guide. At Aberdeen
the high tide does not appear till an hour later
than the doctrine would suggest. It is two hours
late at London, three at Tynemouth, four at Tralee,
five at Sligo, and six at Hull. This last port
would be indeed the haven of refuge for those
who believe that the low tide ought to be under
the moon. At Hull this is no doubt the case; and
if at all other places the water behaved as it does
at Hull, why then, of course, it would follow that
the law of low water under the moon was generally
true. But then this would not tally with the condition of affairs at the other places I have named;
and to complete the cycle I shall add a few more.
At Bristol the high water does not get up until
seven hours after the moon has passed the meridian,
at Arklow the delay is eight hours, at Yarmouth
it is nine, at the Needles it is ten hours, while
lastly, the moon has nearly got back to the
meridian again ere it has succeeded in dragging

up the tide on which Liverpool's great commerce so largely depends.

Nor does the result of studying the tides along other coasts beside our own decide more conclusively on the mooted point. Even ports in the vast ocean give a very uncertain response. Kerguelen Island and Santa Cruz might seem to prove that the high tide occurs under the moon, but unfortunately both Fiji and Ascension seem to present us with an equally satisfactory demonstration, that beneath the moon is the invariable home of low water.

I do not mean to say that the study of the tides is in other respects such a confused subject as the facts I have stated would seem to indicate. It becomes rather puzzling, no doubt, when we compare the tides at one port with the tides elsewhere. The law and order are, then, by no means conspicuous, they are often hardly discernible. But when we confine our attention to the tides at a single port, the problem becomes at once a very intelligible one. Indeed, the investigation of the tides is an easy subject, if we are contented with a reasonably approximate solution ; should, however, it be necessary to discuss fully the tides at any port, the theory of the method necessary for doing so is available, and an interesting and beautiful theory it certainly is.

Let us then speak for a few moments about the methods by which we can study the tides at a particular port. The principle on which it is based is a very simple one.

It is the month of August, the 18th, we shall suppose, and we are going to enjoy a delicious swim in the sea. We desire, of course, to secure a high tide for the purpose of doing so, and we call an almanac to help us. I refer to the Thom's Dublin Directory, where I find the tide to be high at 10h. 14m. on the morning of the 18th of August. That will then be the time to go down to the baths at Howth or Kingstown.

But what I am now going to discourse to you about is not the delights of sea-bathing, it is rather a different inquiry. I want to ask, How did the people who prepared that almanac know years beforehand, that on that particular day the tide would be high at that particular hour? How do they predict for every day the hour of high water?

and how comes it to pass that these predictions are invariably correct ?

We first refer to that wonderful book, the *Nautical Almanac*. In that volume the movements of the moon are set forth with full detail ; and among other particulars we can learn on page iv of every month the mean time of the moon's meridian passage. It appears that on the day in question the moon crossed the meridian at 11h. 23m. Thus we see there was high water at Dublin at 10h. 14m., and 1h. 9m. later, that is, at 11h. 23m., the moon crossed the meridian.

Let us take another instance. There is a high tide at 3.40 P.M. on the 25th August, and again the infallible *Nautical Almanac* tells us that the moon crossed the meridian at 5h. 44m., that is, at 2h. 4m. after the high water.

In the first case the moon followed the tide in about an hour, and in the second case the moon followed in about two hours. Now if we are to be satisfied with a very rough tide rule for Dublin, we may say generally that there is always a high tide an hour and a half before the moon crosses the meridian. This would not be a very accurate rule, but I can assure you of this, that if you go by it you will never fail of finding a good tide to enable you to enjoy your swim. I do not say this rule would enable you to construct a respectable tide-table. A ship-owner who has to creep up the river, and to whom the inches of water are often material, will require far more accurate tables than this simple rule could give. But we enter into rather complicated matters when we attempt to give any really accurate methods of computation. On these we shall say a few words presently. What I first want to do, is to impress upon you in a simple way the fact of the relation between the tide and the moon.

To give another illustration, let us see how the tides at London Bridge are related to the moon. On Jan. 1st, 1887, it appeared that the tide was high at 6h. 26m. P.M., and that the moon had crossed the meridian 56m. previously; on the 8th Jan. the tide was high at 0h. 43m. P.M., and the moon had crossed the meridian 2h. 1m. previously. Therefore we would have at London Bridge high water following the moon's transit in somewhere about an hour and a half.

I choose a day at random, for example—the 12th April. The moon crosses the upper meridian at 3h. 39m. A.M., and the lower meridian at 4h 6m. P.M. Adding an hour and a half to each would give the high tides at 5h. 9m. A.M. and 5h. 36m. P.M.; as a matter of fact, they are 4h. 58m. A.M. and 5h. 20m. P.M.

But these illustrations are sufficient. We find that at London, in a general way, high water appears at London Bridge about an hour and a half after the moon has passed the meridian of London. It so happens that the interval at Dublin is about the same, *i.e.* an hour and a half; only that in the latter case the high water precedes the moon by that interval instead of following it. We may employ the same simple process at other places. Choose two days about a week distant; find· on each occasion the interval between the transit of the moon and the time of high water, then the mean of these two differences will always give some notion of the interval between high water and the moon's transit. If then we take from the *Nautical Almanac* the time of the moon's transit, and apply to it the correction proper for the port, we shall always have a sufficiently good tide-table to guide us in choosing a suitable time for taking our swim or our walk by the sea-side; though if you be the captain of a vessel, you will not be so imprudent as to enter port without taking counsel of the accurate tide-tables, for which we are indebted to the Admiralty.

Every one who visits the sea-side, or who lives at a sea-port, should know this constant for the tides, which affect him and his movements so materially. If he will discover it from his own experience, so much the better.

The first point to be ascertained is the time of high water. Do not take this from any local table; you ought to observe it for yourself. You will go to the pier head, or, better still, to some place where the rise and fall of the mere waves of the sea will not embarrass you in your work. You must note by your watch the time when the tide is highest. An accurate way of doing this will be to have a scale on which you can measure the height at intervals of five minutes about the time of high water. You will then be able to conclude the time at which the tide was actually at its highest point; but even if no great accuracy be obtainable, you can still get much interesting information, for you will without much difficulty be right within ten minutes or a quarter of an hour.

The correction for the port is properly called the "establishment," this being the average time of high water on the days of full and change of the moon at the particular port in question.

We can considerably amend the elementary notion of the tides which the former method has given us, if we adopt the plan described by Dr. Whewell in the first four editions of the *Admiralty Manual of Scientific Inquiry.* We speak of the interval between the transit of the moon and the time of high water as the luni-tidal interval. Of course at full and change this is the same thing as the establishment, but for other phases of the moon the establishment must receive a correction before being used as the luni-tidal interval. The correction is given by the following table—

Hour of Moon's transit after Sun :

0	1	2	3	4	5	6	7	8	9	10	11
0	−20m	−30m	−50m	−60m	−60m	−60m	−40m	−10m	+10m	+20m	+10m

Correction of establishment to find luni-tidal interval :

Thus at a port where the establishment was 3h. 25m., let us suppose that the transit of the moon took place at 6 P.M.; then we correct the establishment by —60m., and find the luni-tidal interval to be 2h. 25m., and accordingly the high water takes place at 8h. 25m. P.M.

But even this method is only an approximation. The study of the tides is based on accurate observation of their rise and fall on different places round the earth. To show how these observations are to be made, and how they are to be discussed and reduced when they have been made, I may refer to the last edition of the *Admiralty Manual of Scientific Inquiry*, 1886. For a complete study of the tides at any port a self-registering tide-gauge should be erected, on which not alone the heights and times of high and low water should be depicted, but also the continuous curve which shows at any time the height of the water. In fact, the whole subject of the practical observation and discussion and prediction of tides is full of valuable instruction, and may be cited as one of the most complete examples of the modern scientific methods.

In the first place, the tide-gauge itself is a

delicate instrument ; it is actuated by a float which rises and falls with the water, due provision being made that the mere influence of waves shall not make it to oscillate inconveniently. The motion of the float when suitably reduced by mechanism serves to guide a pencil, which, acting on the paper round a revolving drum, gives a faithful and un-intermitting record of the height of the water.

Thus what the tide-gauge does is to present to us a long curved line of which the summits corre-spond to the heights of high water, while the depressions are the corresponding points of low water. The long undulations of this curve are, how-ever, very irregular. At spring tides, when the sun and the moon conspire, the elevations rise much higher and the depressions sink much lower than they do at neap tides, when the high water raised by the moon is reduced by the action of the sun. There are also many minor irregularities which show the tides to be not nearly such simple phe-nomena as might be at first supposed. But what we might hastily think of as irregularities are, in truth, the most interesting parts of the whole phenomena. Just as in the observations of the planets the study of the perturbations has led us to results of the widest interest and instruction, so it is these minor phenomena of the tides which seem most pregnant with scientific interest.

The tide-gauge gives us an elaborate curve. How are we to interpret that curve? Here a beautiful mathematical theorem fortunately comes to our aid. Just as ordinary sounds consist of a number of undulations blended together, so the tidal wave consists of a number of distinct undulations superposed. Of these the ordinary lunar tide and the ordinary solar tide are the two principal; but there are also minor undulations, harmonics, so to speak, some originating from the moon, some originating from the sun, and some from both bodies acting in concert.

In the study of sound we can employ an acoustic apparatus for the purpose of decomposing any proposed note, and finding not only the main undulation itself, but the several superposed harmonics which give to the note its timbre. So also we can analyze the undulation of the tide, and show the component parts. The decomposition is effected by the process known as

C

harmonic analysis. The principle of the method
may be very simply described. Let us fix our attention on any particular "tide," for so the various
elements are denoted. We can always determine
beforehand, with as much accuracy as we may
require, what the period of that tide will be. For
instance, the period of the lunar semi-diurnal tide
will of course be half the average time occupied
by the moon in travelling round from the meridian
of any place until it regains the same meridian ;
the period of the lunar diurnal tide will be
double as great ; and there are fortnightly tides,
and others of periods still greater. The essential
point to notice is, that the periods of these tides
are given by purely astronomical considerations,
and do not depend upon the actual observations of
the height of the water.

We measure off on the curve the height of the
tide at intervals of an hour. The larger the
number of such measures that are available the
better ; but even if there be only three hundred
and sixty or seven hundred and twenty consecu-
tive hours, then, as shown by Professor G. H.
Darwin in the *Admiralty Manual* already referred

to, it will still be possible to obtain a very competent knowledge of the tides in the particular port where the gauge has been placed.

The art (for such indeed it may be described) of harmonic analysis consists in deducing from the hourly observations the facts with regard to each of the constituent tides. This art has been carried to such perfection, that it has been reduced to a very simple series of arithmetical operations. Indeed it has now been found possible to call in the aid of ingenious mechanism, by which the labours of computation are entirely superseded. The pointer of the harmonic analyzer has merely to be traced over the curve which the tide-gauge has drawn, and it is the function of the machine to decompose the composite undulation into its parts, and to exhibit the several constituent tides whose confluence gives the total result.

As if nothing should be left to complete the perfection of a process which, both from its theoretical and its practical sides, is of such importance, a machine for predicting tides has been designed, constructed, and is now in ordinary use. When by the aid of the harmonic analysis the effectiveness of the several constituent tides affecting a port have become fully determined, it is of course possible to predict the tides for that port. Each " tide " is a simple periodic rise and fall, and we can compute for any future time the height of each were it acting alone. These heights can all be added together, and thus the height of the water is obtained. In this way a tide-table is formed, and such a table when complete will express not alone the hours and heights of high water on every day, but the height of the water at any intervening hour.

The computations necessary for this purpose are no doubt simple, so far as their principle is concerned ; but they are exceedingly tedious, and any process must be welcomed which affords mitigation of a task so laborious. The theory of the tides owes much to Sir William Thomson in the methods of observation and in the methods of reduction. He has now completed the practical parts of the subject by inventing and constructing the famous tide-predicting engine.

The principle of this engine is comparatively simple. There is a chain which at one end is fixed, and at the other end carries the pencil which is pressed against the revolving drum on which the prediction is to be inscribed. Between its two ends the chain passes up and down over pulleys. Each pulley corresponds to one of the "tides," and there are about a dozen altogether, some of which exercise but little effect. Of course if the centres of the pulleys were all fixed the pen could not move, but the centre of each pulley describes a circle with a radius proportional to the amplitude of the corresponding tide, and in a time proportional to the period of that tide. When these pulleys are all set so as to start at the proper phases, the motion is produced by turning round a handle which sets all the pulleys in motion, and makes the drum rotate. The tide curve is thus rapidly drawn out; and so expeditious is the machine, that the tides of a port for an entire year can be completely worked out in a couple of hours.

While the student or the philosopher who seeks to render any account of the tide on dynamical grounds is greatly embarrassed by the difficulties introduced by friction, we, for our present purpose

in the study of the great romance of modern
science opened up to us by the theory of the tides,
have to welcome friction as the agent which gives
to the tides their significance from our point of
view.

There is the greatest difference between the
height of the rise and fall of the tide at different
localities. Out in mid-ocean, for instance, an island
like St. Helena is washed by a tide only about
three feet in range; an enclosed sea like the
Caspian is subject to no appreciable tides whatever,
while the Mediterranean, notwithstanding its connection with the Atlantic, is still only subject to
very inconsiderable tides, varying from one foot to
a few feet. The statement that water always finds
its own level must be received, like many another
proposition in nature, with a considerable degree of
qualification. Long ere one tide could have found
its way through the Straits of Gibraltar in sufficient
volume to have appreciably affected the level of the
great inland sea, its effects would have been obli-
terated by succeeding tides. On the other hand,
there are certain localities which expose a funnel-
shape opening to the sea; into these the great tidal

wave rushes, and as it passes onwards towards the
narrow part, the waters become piled up so as to
produce tidal phenomena of abnormal proportions.
Thus, in our own islands, we have in the Bristol
Channel a wide mouth into which a great tide
enters, and as it hurries up the Severn it produces
the extraordinary phenomenon of the Bore.   The
Bristol Channel also concentrates the great wave
which gives Chepstow and Cardiff a tidal range of
thirty-seven or thirty-eight feet at springs, and
forces the sea up the river Avon so as to give
Bristol a wonderful tide.   There is hardly any
more interesting spot in our islands for the observation of tides than is found on Clifton Suspension
Bridge.   From that beautiful structure you look
down on a poor and not very attractive stream,
which two hours later becomes transformed into a
river of ample volume, down which great ships are
navigated.   But of all places in the world, the most
colossal tidal phenomena are those in the Bay of
Fundy.   Here the Atlantic passes into a long
channel whose sides gradually converge.   When
the great pulse of the tide rushes up this channel,
it is gradually accumulated into a mighty volume

at the upper end, the ebb and flow of which at spring tides extends through an astonishing range of more than fifty feet.

The discrepancies between the tides at different places are chiefly due to the local formations of the coasts and the sea-beds. Indeed, it seems that if the whole earth were covered with an uniform and deep ocean of water, the tides would be excessively feeble. On no other supposition can we reasonably account for the fact that our barometric records fail to afford us any very distinct evidence as to the existence of tides in the atmosphere. For you will, of course, remember that our atmosphere may be regarded as a deep and vast ocean of air, which embraces the whole earth, extending far above the loftiest summits of the mountains.

It is one of the profoundest of nature's laws that wherever friction takes place, energy has to be consumed. Perhaps I ought rather to say transformed, for of course it is now well known that consumption of energy in the sense of absolute loss is impossible. Thus, when energy is expended in moving a body in opposition to the force of friction, or in agitating a liquid, the energy which disappears in its mechanical form reappears in the form of heat. The agitation of water by paddles moving through it warms the water, and the accession of heat thus acquired measures the energy which has been expended in making the paddles rotate. The motion of a liquid of which the particles move among each other with friction, can only be sustained by the incessant degradation of energy from the mechanical form into the lower form of diffused heat. Thus the very fact that the tides are ebbing and flowing, and that there is consequently incessant friction going on among all the particles of water in the ocean, shows us that there must be some great store of energy constantly available to supply the incessant draughts made upon it by the daily oscillation of the tides. In addition to the mere friction between the particles of water, there are also many other ways in which the tides proclaim to us that there is some great hoard of energy which is continually accessible to their wants. Stand on the bank of an estuary or river up and down which a great tidal current ebbs and flows; you will see the water copiously charged with sediment which the tide is bearing along. Engineers are well aware of the potency of the tide as a vehicle for transporting stupendous quantities of sand or mud. A sand-bank impedes the navigation of a river; the removal of that sand-bank would be a task, perhaps, conceivably possible by the use of steam dredges and other appliances, whereby vast quantities of sand could be raised and transported to where they can be safely deposited in deep water. It is sometimes possible to effect the desired end by applying the power of the tide. A sea-wall judiciously thrown out can be made to concentrate the tide into a much narrower channel. Its daily oscillations will be accomplished with greater vehemence, and as the tide rushes furiously backwards and forwards over the obstacle, the incessant action will gradually remove it, and the impediment to navigation may be cleared away. Here we actually see the tides performing a piece of definite and very laborious work, to accomplish which by the more ordinary agents would be a stupendous task.

In some places the tides are actually harnessed so as to accomplish useful work. I have read that

underneath old London Bridge there used formerly
to be great water-wheels, which were turned by
the tide as it rushed up the river, and turned again,
though in the opposite way, by the ebbing tide.
These wheels were, I believe, employed to pump up
water, though it does not seem obvious for what
purposes the water would have been suitable.
Indeed in the ebb and flow all round our coasts
there is a potential source of energy which has
generally been allowed to run to waste, save perhaps in one or two places in the south of England.
The tide could be utilized in various ways. Many of
you will remember the floating mills on the Rhine.
They are vessels like paddle steamers anchored in
the rapid current. The flow of the river makes the
paddles rotate, and thus the machinery in the
interior is worked. Such craft moored in a rapid
tide-way could also be made to convey the power
of the tides into the mechanism of the mill. Or there
is still another method which has been employed,
and which will perhaps have a future before it in
those approaching times when the coal-cellars of
England shall be exhausted. Imagine on the sea-
coast a large flat extent which is inundated twice
every day by the tide. Let us build a stout

wall round this area, and provide it with a sluice-gate. Open the gate as the tide rises, and the great pond will be filled; then at the moment of high water close the sluice, and the pond-full will be impounded. If at low tide the sluice be opened the water will rush tumultuously out. Now suppose that a water-wheel be provided, so that the rapid rush of water from the exit shall fall upon its blades; then a source of power is obviously the result.

At present, however, such a contrivance would find but few advocates, for of course the commercial aspect of the question is that which will decide whether the scheme is practicable and economical. The issue indeed can be very simply stated. Suppose that a given quantity of power be required—let us say that of one hundred horse. Then we have to consider the conditions under which a contrivance of the kind we have sketched shall yield a power of this amount. Sir William Thomson, in a very interesting address to the British Association at York in 1881, discussed this question, and I shall here make use of the facts he brought forward on that occasion. He showed that to obtain as much power as could be produced by a steam-engine of one hundred horse power, a very large reservoir would be required. It is doubtful indeed whether there would be many localities on the earth which would be suitable for the purpose. Suppose, however, an estuary could be found which had an area of forty acres; then if a wall were thrown across the mouth so that the tide could be impounded, the total amount of power that could be yielded by a water-wheel worked by the incessant influx and efflux of the tide would be equal to that yielded by the one hundred horse engine, running continuously from one end of the year to the other.

There are many drawbacks to a tide-mill of this description. In the first place, its situation would naturally be far removed from other conveniences necessary for manufacturing purposes. Then too there is the great irregularity in the way in which the power is rendered available. At certain periods during the twenty-four hours the mill would stop running, and the hours when this happened would be constantly changing. The inconvenience from the manufacturer's point of view of a deficiency of power during neap tides might not be compensated by the fact that he had an excessive supply of power at spring-tides. Before tide-mills could be suitable for manufacturing purposes, some means must be found for storing away the energy when it is redundant, and applying it when its presence is required. We should want in fact for great sources of energy some contrivance which should fulfil the same function as the accumulators do in an electrical installation.

Even then, however, the financial consideration remains, as to whether the cost of building the dam and maintaining the tide-mill in good order will not on the whole exceed the original price and the charges for the maintenance of a hundred horse power steam-engine. There cannot be a doubt that in this epoch of the earth's history, so long as the price of coal is only a few shillings a ton, the tide-mill, even though we seem to get its power without current expense, is vastly more expensive than a steam-engine. Indeed, Sir William Thomson remarks, that wherever a suitable tidal basin could be found, it would be nearly as easy to reclaim the land altogether from the sea. And if

this were in any locality where manufactures were
possible, the commercial value of forty acres of re-
claimed land would greatly exceed all the expenses
attending the steam-engine. But when the time
comes, as come it apparently will, that the price of
coal shall have risen to several pounds a ton, the
economical aspect of steam as compared with other
prime movers will be greatly altered; it will then
no doubt be found advantageous to utilize great
sources of energy, such as Niagara and the tides,
which it is now more prudent to let run to waste.

For my argument, however, it matters little that
the tides are not constrained to do much useful
work. They are always doing work of some kind,
whether that be merely heating the particles of
water by friction, or vaguely transporting sand
from one part of the ocean to the other. Useful
work or useless work are alike from the present
point of view. We know that work can never be
done unless by the consumption or transformation
of energy. For each unit of work that is done—
whether by any machine or contrivance, by the
muscles of man or any other animal, by the winds,
the waves, or the tides, or in any other way

whatever—a certain equivalent quantity of energy must have been expended. When, therefore, we see any work being performed, we may always look for the source of energy to which the machine owes its efficiency. Every machine illustrates the old story, that perpetual motion is impossible. A mechanical device, however ingenious may be the construction, or however accurate the workmanship, can never possess what is called perpetual motion. It is needless to enter into details of any proposed contrivance of wheels, of pumps, of pulleys; it is sufficient to say that nothing in the shape of mechanism can work without friction, that friction produces heat, that heat is a form of energy, and that to replace the energy consumed in producing the heat there must be some source from which the machine is replenished if its motion is to be continued indefinitely.

Hence, as the tides may be regarded as a machine doing work, we have to ascertain the origin of that energy which they are continually expending. It is at this point that we first begin to feel the difficulties inherent in the theory of tidal evolution. I do not mean difficulties in the sense of doubts, for

up to the present I have mentioned no doubtful
point. When I come to such I shall give due
warning. By difficulties I now mean points which
it is not easy to understand without a little dynamical theory ; but we must face these difficulties,
and endeavour to elucidate them as well as we
can.

Let us first see what the sources of energy can
possibly be on which the tides are permitted to
draw. Our course is simplified by the fact that
the energy of which we have to speak is of a
mechanical description, that is to say, not involving heat or other more obscure forms of
energy. A simple type of energy is that possessed by a clock-weight after the clock has been
wound. A store of power is thus laid up which
is gradually doled out during the week in small
quantities, second by second, to sustain the
motion of the pendulum. The energy in this case
is due to the fact that the weight is attracted by
the earth, and is yielded according as the weight
sinks downwards. In the separation between two
mutually attracting bodies, a store of energy is
thus implied. What we learn from an ordinary

D

clock may be extended to the great bodies of the universe. The moon is a gigantic globe separated from our earth by a distance of 240,000 miles. The attraction between these two bodies always tends to bring them together. No doubt the moon is not falling towards the earth as the descending clock-weight is doing. We may, in fact, consider the moon, so far as our present object is concerned, to be revolving almost in a circle, of which the earth is the centre. If the moon, however, were to be stopped, it would at once commence to rush down towards the earth, whither it would arrive with an awful crash in the course of four or five days. It is fortunately true that the moon does not behave thus; but it has the ability of doing so, and thus the mere separation between the earth and the moon involves the existence of a stupendous quantity of energy, capable under certain conditions of undergoing transformation.

There is also another source of mechanical energy besides that we have just referred to. A rapidly moving body possesses, in virtue of its motion, a store of readily available energy, and it is easy to show that energy of this type is capable of trans-

formation into other **types.** Think of a cannon-
ball rushing through the air at a speed of a thousand
feet per second ; it is capable of wreaking disaster
wherever its blow **may fall,** simply because its
rapid **motion** is the vehicle **by** which **the** energy
of the gunpowder is **transferred from the gun** to
where the blow is **to be struck.** Had the **cannon**
been directed vertically **upwards,** then **the pro-**
jectile, leaving the muzzle **with the same initial**
velocity as before, **would soar up and** up, **with**
gradually abating speed, **until at last it** reached **a**
turning-point, the elevation **of which** would depend
upon the initial velocity. Poised for **a** moment at
the summit, the cannon-ball **may** then be likened
to **the** clock-weight, **for** the **entire energy which**
it possessed **by its** motion has **been transformed**
into the statical **energy of a raised weight.** Thus
we see these two forms **of energy are mutually**
interchangeable. **The raised weight if allowed to**
fall will acquire velocity, **or the** rapidly **moving**
weight if directed upwards will acquire **altitude.**

The quantity of energy which can **be** conveyed
by a rapidly moving body increases greatly with
its speed. For instance, if the speed of the body

D 2

be doubled, the energy will be increased fourfold, or, in general, the energy which a moving body possesses may be said to be proportional to the square of its speed. Here then we have another source of the energy present in our earth-moon system; for the moon is hurrying along in its path with a speed of two-thirds of a mile per second, or about twice or three times the speed of a cannon-shot. Hence the fact that the moon is continuously revolving in a circle shows us that it possesses a store of energy which is nine times as great as that which a cannon-ball as massive as the moon, and fired with the ordinary velocity, would receive from the powder which discharged it.

Thus we see that the moon is endowed with two sources of energy, one of which is due to its separation from the earth, and the other to the speed of its motion. Though these are distinct, they are connected together by a link which it is important for us to comprehend. The speed with which the moon revolves around the earth is connected with the moon's distance from the earth. The moon might, for instance, revolve in a larger circle than that which it actually pursues; but if it did so, the speed of its motion would have to be appropriately lessened. The orbit of the moon might have a much smaller radius than it has at present, provided that the speed was sufficiently increased to compensate for the increased attraction which the earth would exercise at the lessened distance. Indeed, I am here only stating what every one is familiar with under the form of Kepler's Law, that the square of the periodic time is in proportion to the cube of the mean distance. To each distance of the moon therefore belongs an appropriate speed. The energy due to the moon's position and the energy due to its motion are therefore connected together. One of these quantities cannot be altered without the other undergoing change. If the moon's orbit were increased there would be a gain of energy due to the enlarged distance, and a loss of energy due to the diminished speed. These would not, however, exactly compensate. On the whole, we may represent the total energy of the moon as a single quantity, which increases when the distance of the moon from the earth increases, and lessens when the distance from the earth to the moon

lessens. For simplicity we may speak of this as
moon-energy.

But the most important constituent of the store
of energy in the earth-moon system is that contributed by the earth itself. I do not now speak
of the energy due to the velocity of the earth in
its orbit round the sun. The moon indeed partici-
pates in this equally with the earth, but it does
not affect those mutual actions between the earth
and moon with which we are at present concerned.
We are, in fact, discussing the action of that piece
of machinery the earth-moon system ; and its
action is not affected by the circumstance that
the entire machine is being bodily transported
around the sun in a great annual voyage. This
has little more to do with our present argument
than has the fact that a man is walking about to
do with the motions of the works of the watch in
his pocket. We shall, however, have to allude to
this subject further on.

The energy of the earth which is significant in
the earth-moon theory is due to the earth's rotation upon its axis. We may here again use as
an illustration the action of machinery ; and the

special contrivance that I now refer to is the
punching-engine that is used in our ship-building
works. In preparing a plate of iron to be riveted
to the side of a ship, a number of holes have to be
made all round the margin of the plate. These
holes must be half an inch or more in diameter,
and the plate is sometimes as much as, or more
than, half an inch in thickness. The holes are produced in the metal by forcing a steel punch through
it ; and this is accomplished without even heating
the plate so as to soften the iron. It is needless to
say that an intense force must be applied to the
punch. On the other hand, the distance through
which the punch has to be moved is comparatively
small. The punch is attached to the end of a
powerful lever, the other end of the lever is raised
by a cam, so as to depress the punch to do its
work. An essential part of the machine is a small
but heavy fly-wheel connected by gearing with
the cam.

This fly-wheel when rapidly revolving contains within it, in virtue of its motion, a large
store of energy which has gradually accumulated
during the time that the punch is not in action.

The energy is no doubt originally supplied from a steam-engine. What we are especially concerned with is the action of the rapidly rotating wheel as a reservoir in which a large store of energy can be conveniently maintained until such time as it is wanted. In the action of punching, when the steel die comes down upon the surface of the plate, a large quantity of energy is suddenly demanded to force the punch against the intense resistance it experiences; the energy for this purpose is drawn from the store in the fly-wheel, which experiences no doubt a check in its velocity, to be restored again from the energy of the engine during the interval which elapses before the punch is called on to make the next hole.

Another illustration of the fly-wheel on a splendid scale is to be seen in steel works, where railway lines are being manufactured. A white-hot ingot of steel is presented to a pair of powerful rollers, which grip the steel, and send it through at the other side both compressed and elongated. Tremendous power is required to meet the sudden demand on the machine at the critical moment. To obtain this power an engine of immense

horse-power is sometimes attached directly to the
rollers, but more frequently an engine of rather less
horse-power will be used, the might of this engine
being applied to giving rapid rotation to a fly-
wheel, which may thus be regarded as a reservoir
full of energy. The rolling mills then obtain from
this store in the fly-wheel whatever energy is
necessary for their gigantic task

These illustrations will suffice to show how a
rapidly rotating body may contain energy in
virtue of its rotation, just as a cannon-ball contains
energy in virtue of its speed of translation, or as
a clock-weight has energy in virtue of the fact
that it has some distance to fall before it reaches
the earth. The rotating body need not necessarily
have the shape of a wheel—it may be globular in
form ; nor need the axes of rotation be fixed in
bearings, like those of the fly-wheel ; nor of course
is there any limit to the dimensions which the
rotating body may assume. Our earth is, in fact,
a vast rotating body 8000 miles in diameter, and
turning round upon its axis once every twenty-
three hours and fifty-six minutes. Viewed in this
way, the earth is to be regarded as a gigantic

fly-wheel containing a quantity of energy great in correspondence with the earth's mass. The amount of energy which can be stored by rotation also depends upon the square of the velocity with which the body turns round; thus if our earth turned round in half the time which it does at present, that is, if the day was twelve hours instead of twenty-four hours, the energy contained in virtue of that rotation would be four times its present amount.

Reverting now to the earth-moon system, the energy which that system contains consists essentially of two parts—the moon-energy, whose composite character I have already explained, and the earth-energy, which has its origin solely in the rotation of the earth on its axis. It is necessary to observe that these are essentially distinct—there is no necessary relation between the speed of the earth's rotation and the distance of the moon, such as there is between the distance of the moon and the speed with which it revolves in its orbit.

For completeness, it ought to be added that there is also some energy due to the moon's rotation on its axis, but this is very small for two

reasons: first, because the moon is small compared
with the earth, and second, because the angular
velocity of the moon is also very small compared
with that of the earth. We may therefore dismiss
as insignificant the contributions from this source
to the sum total of energy.

I have frequently used illustrations derived from
machinery, but I want now to emphasize the
profound distinction that exists between the rotation
of the earth and the rotation of a fly-wheel in
a machine shop. They are both, no doubt, energy-
holders, but it must be borne in mind, that as the
fly-wheel doles out its energy to supply the wants
of the machines with which it is connected, a resti-
tution of its store is continually going on by the
action of the engine, so that on the whole the
speed of the fly-wheel does not slacken. The
earth, however, must be likened to a fly-wheel
which has been disconnected with the engine. If,
therefore, the earth have to supply certain demands
on its accumulation of energy, it can only do so
by a diminution of its hoard, and this involves a
sacrifice of some of its speed.

In the earth-moon system there is no engine

at hand to restore the losses of energy which are inevitable when work has to be done. But we have seen that work is done; we have shown, in fact, that the tides are at present doing work, and have been doing work for as long a period in the past as our imagination can extend to. The energy which this work has necessitated can only have been drawn from the existing store in the system ; that energy consists of two parts—the moon-energy and the earth's rotation energy. The problem therefore for us to consider is, which of these two banks the tides have drawn on to meet their constant expenditure. This is not a question that can be decided offhand ; in fact, if we attempt to decide it in an offhand manner we shall certainly go wrong. It seems so very plausible to say that as the moon causes the tides, therefore the energy which these tides expend should be contributed by the moon. But this is not the case. It actually happens that though the moon does cause the tides, yet when those tides consume energy they draw it not from the distant moon, but from the vast supply which they find ready to their hand, stored up in the rotation of the earth.

The demonstration of this is not a very simple matter; in fact, it is so far from being simple that many philosophers, including some eminent ones too, while admitting that of course the tides must have drawn their energy from one or other or both of these two sources, yet found themselves unable to assign how the demand was distributed between the two conceivable sources of supply.

We are indebted to Professor Purser of Belfast for having indicated the true dynamical principle on which the problem depends. It involves reasoning based simply on the laws of motion and on elementary mathematics, but not in the least involving questions of astronomical observation. It would be impossible for me in a lecture like this to give any explanation of the mathematical principles referred to. I shall, however, endeavour by some illustrations to set before you what this profound principle really is. Were I to give it the old name I should call it the law of the conservation of areas; the more modern writers, however, speak of it as the conservation of moment of momentum, an expression which exhibits the nature of the principle in a more definite manner.

I do not see how to give any very accurate
illustration of what this law means, but I must
make the attempt, and if you think the illustration
beneath the dignity of the subject, I can only
plead the difficulty of mathematics as an excuse.
Let us suppose that a ball-room is fairly filled
with dancers, or those willing to dance, and that
a merry waltz is being played; the couples have
formed, and the floor is occupied with pairs who
are whirling round and round in that delightful
amusement. Some couples drop out for a while
and others strike in; the fewer couples there are
the wider is the range around which they can
waltz, the more numerous the couples the less
individual range will they possess. I want you to
realize that in the progress of the dance there is
a certain total quantity of spin at any moment
in progress; this spin is partly made up of the
rotation by which each dancer revolves round his
partner, and partly of the circular orbit about the
room which each couple endeavours to describe.
If there are too many couples on the floor for the
general enjoyment of the dance, then both the orbit
and the angular velocity of each couple will be

restricted by the interference with their neighbours.
We may, however, **assert** that so long as the dance
is in full swing the total quantity of spin, partly
rotational and partly orbital, will remain constant.
When there are but few couples the unimpeded
rotation and the large orbits will produce as much
spin as when there is a much larger **number** of
couples, for in the latter case **the** diminished
freedom will lessen the quantity of spin produced
by each individual **pair.** It will sometimes happen
too **that** collision **will** take place, but the slight
diversions thus arising only increase the general
merriment, so that the total quantity of spin may
be sustained, even though one **or** two couples
are placed temporarily *hors de combat.* **I have**
invoked **a** ball-room for the purpose of **bringing**
out what **we** may call the law of **the** conservation
of spin. No matter how much the individual per-
formers may change, or no matter what vicissitudes arise from their collision and other mutual
actions, yet the total quantity of spin remains
unchanged.

Let us look at the earth-moon system. The
law of the conservation of moment of momentum

may, with sufficient accuracy for our present purpose, be interpreted to mean that the total quantity of spin in the system remains unaltered. In our system the spin is threefold; there is first the rotation of the earth on its axis, there is the rotation of the moon on its axis, and then there is the orbital revolution of the moon around the earth. The law to which we refer asserts that the total quantity of these three spins, each estimated in the proper way, will remain unaltered. It matters not that tides may ebb and flow, or that the distribution of the spin shall vary, but its total amount remains inflexibly constant. One constituent of the total amount—that is, the rotation of the moon on its axis—is so insignificant, that for our present purposes it may be entirely disregarded. We may therefore assert that the amount of spin in the earth, due to its rotation round its axis, added to the amount of spin in the moon due to its revolution round the earth, remains unalterable. If one of these quantities change by increase or by decrease, the other must correspondingly change by decrease or by increase. If, therefore, from any cause, the earth began to spin a little

more quickly round its axis, the moon must do a
little less spin; and consequently, it must shorten
its distance from the earth. Or suppose that the
earth's velocity of rotation is abated, then its contribution to the total amount of spin is lessened;
the deficiency must therefore be made up by the
moon, but this can only be done by an enlargement of the moon's orbit. I should add, as a
caution, that these results are true only on the
supposition that the earth-moon system is isolated
from all external interference. With this proviso,
however, it matters not what may happen to the
earth or moon, or what influence one of them may
exert upon the other, no matter what tides may
be raised, no matter even if the earth fly into
fragments, the whole quantity of spin of all those
fragments would, if added to the spin of the
moon, yield the same unalterable total. We are
here in possession of a most valuable dynamical
principle. We are not concerned with any special
theory as to the action of the tides; it is sufficient
for us that in some way or other the tides have
been caused by the moon, and that being so, the
principle of the conservation of spin will apply.

E

Were the earth and the moon both rigid bodies, then there could be of course no tides on the earth, for if rigid it is devoid of ocean. The rotation of the earth on its axis would therefore be absolutely without change, and therefore the necessary condition of the conservation of spin would be very simply attained by the fact that neither of the constituent parts changed. The earth, however, not being entirely rigid, and being subject to tides, this simple state of things cannot continue; there must be some change in progress.

I have already shown that the fact of the ebbing and the flowing of the tide necessitates an expenditure of energy, and we saw that this energy must come either from that stored up in the earth by its rotation, or from that possessed by the moon in virtue of its distance and revolution. The law of the conservation of spin will enable us to decide at once as to whence the tides get their energy. Suppose they took it from the moon, the moon would then lose in energy, and consequently come nearer the earth. The quantity of spin contributed by the moon would therefore be lessened, and accordingly the spin to be made up by the earth would be increased. That means, of course, that the velocity of the earth rotating on its axis must be increased, and this again would necessitate an increase in the earth's rotational energy. It can be shown, too, that to keep the total spin right, the energy of the earth would have to gain more than the moon would have lost by revolving in a smaller orbit. Thus we find that the total quantity of energy in the system would be increased. This would lead to the absurd result that the action of the tides manufactured energy in our system. Of course, such a doctrine cannot be true; it would amount to a perpetual motion! We might as well try to get a steam-engine which would produce enough heat by friction not only to supply its own boilers, but to satisfy the thermal wants of the whole parish. We must therefore adopt the other alternative. The tides do not draw their energy from the moon; they draw it from the store possessed by the earth in virtue of its rotation.

We can now state the end of this rather long discussion in a very simple and brief manner. Energy can only be yielded by the earth at the

E 2

expense of some of the speed of its rotation. The
tides must therefore cause the earth to revolve
more slowly ; in other words, *the tides are increasing
the length of the day.*

The earth therefore loses some of its velocity
of rotation ; consequently it does less than its due
share of the total quantity of spin, and an increased
quantity of spin must therefore be accomplished
by the moon ; but this can only be done by an
enlargement of its orbit. Thus there are two great
consequences of the tides in the earth-moon system
—the days are getting longer, the moon is receding
further.

These points are so important that I shall try
and illustrate them in another way, which will
show, at all events, that one and both of these tidal
phenomena commend themselves to our common
sense. Have we not shown how the tides in their
ebb and flow are incessantly producing friction,
and have we not also likened the earth to a great
wheel? When the driver wants to stop a railway
train the brakes are put on, and the brake is merely
a contrivance for applying friction to the circumference of a wheel for the purpose of checking its

motion. Or when a great weight is being lowered
by a crane, the motion is checked by a band which
applies friction on the circumference of a wheel
arranged for the special purpose. Need we then
be surprised that the friction of the tides acts like
a brake on the earth, and gradually tends to check
its mighty rotation? The progress of lengthening
the day by the tides is thus readily intelligible. It
is not quite so easy to see why the ebbing and the
flowing of the tide on the earth should actually
have the effect of making the moon to retreat; this
phenomenon is in deference to a profound law of
nature, which tells us that action and reaction are
equal and opposite to each other. If I might
venture on a very homely illustration, I may say
that the moon, like a troublesome fellow, is constantly annoying the earth by dragging its waters
backward and forward by means of tides; and the
earth, to free itself from this irritating interference,
tries to push off the aggressor and to make him
move further away.

Another way in which we can illustrate the
retreat of the moon as the inevitable consequence
of tidal friction is shown in the adjoining figure, in

which the large body
E represents the earth,
and the small body M
the moon. We may for
simplicity regard the
moon as a point, and
as this attracts each
particle of the earth,
the total effect of the
moon on the earth may
be represented by a
single force. By the
law of equality of action
and reaction, the force
of the earth on the
moon is to be repre-
sented by an equal and
opposite force. If there
were no tides then the
moon's force would of
course pass through the
earth's centre; but as the effect of the moon is to
slacken the earth's rotation, it follows that the total
force does not exactly pass through the line of the

earth's centre, but a little to one side, in order to pull the opposite way to that in which the earth is turning, and thus bring down its speed. We may therefore decompose the earth's total force on the moon into two parts, one of which tends directly towards the earth's centre, while the other acts tangentially to the moon's orbit. The central force is of course the main guiding power which keeps the moon in its path; but the incessant tangential force constantly tends to send the moon out further and further, and thus the growth of its orbit can be accounted for.

We therefore conclude finally, that the tides are making the day longer and sending the moon away further. It is the development of the consequences of these laws that specially demands our attention in these lectures. We must have the courage to look at the facts unflinchingly, and deduce from them all the wondrous consequences they involve. Their potency arises from a characteristic feature —they are unintermitting. Most of the great astronomical changes with which we are ordinarily familiar are really periodic: they gradually increase in one direction for years, for centuries, or for untold ages; but then a change comes, and the increase is changed into a decrease, so that after the lapse of becoming periods the original state of things is restored. Such periodic phenomena abound in astronomy. There is the annual fluctuation of the seasons; there is the eighteen or nineteen year period of the moon; there is the great period of the precession of the equinoxes, amounting to twenty-six thousand years; and then there is the stupendous Annus Magnus of hundreds of thousands of years, during which the earth's orbit itself breathes in and out in response to the attraction of the planets. But these periodic phenomena, however important they may be to us mere creatures of a day, are insignificant in their effects on the grand evolution through which the celestial bodies are passing. The really potent agents in fashioning the universe are those which, however slow or feeble they may seem to be, are incessant in their action. The effect which a cause is competent to produce depends not alone upon the intensity of that cause, but also upon the time during which it has been in operation. From the phenomena of geology, as well as from

those of astronomy, we know that this earth and
the system to which it belongs has endured for
ages, not to be counted by scores of thousands of
years, or, as Prof. Tyndall has so well remarked,
" Not for six thousand years, nor for sixty thousand
years, nor six hundred thousand years, but for
æons of untold millions." Those slender agents
which have devoted themselves unceasingly to
the accomplishment of a single task may in this
long lapse of time have accomplished results
of stupendous magnitude. In famed stalactite
caverns we are shown a colossal figure of crystal
extending from floor to roof, and the formation
of that column is accounted for when we see a
tiny drop falling from the roof above to the floor
beneath. A lifetime may not suffice for that falling
drop to add an appreciable increase to the stalactite
down which it trickles, or to the growing stalagmite
on which it fa'ls ; but when the operation has been
in progress for immense ages, it is capable of the
formation of the stately column. Here we have an
illustration of an influence which, though apparently
trivial, acquires colossal significance when adequate
time is afforded. It is phenomena of this kind

which the student of nature should most narrowly
watch, for they are the real architects of the
universe.

The tidal consequences which we have already
demonstrated are emphatically of this non-periodic class—the day is always lengthening, the
moon is always retreating. To-day is longer than
yesterday; to-morrow will be longer than to-day.
It cannot be said that the change is a great one;
it is indeed too small to be appreciable even by
our most delicate observations. In one thousand
years the alteration in the length of a day is only
a small fraction of a second; but what may be a
very small matter in one thousand years can become a very large one in many millions of years.
Thus it is that when we stretch our view through
immense vistas of time past, or when we look forward through immeasurable ages of time to come,
the alteration in the length of the day will assume
the most startling proportions, and involve the
most momentous consequences.

Let us first look back. There was a time when
the day, instead of being the twenty-four hours we
now have, must have been only twenty-three hours,

How many millions of years ago that was I do not pretend to say, nor is the point material for our argument; suffice it to say, that assuming, as geology assures us we may assume, the existence of these æons of millions of years, there was once a time when the day was not only one hour shorter, but was even several hours less than it is at present. Nor need we stop our retrospect at a day of even twenty, or fifteen, or ten hours long; we shall at once project our glance back to an immeasurably remote epoch, at which the earth was spinning round in a time only one sixth or even less of the length of the present day. There is here a reason for our retrospect to halt, for at some eventful period, when the day was about three or four hours long, the earth must have been in a condition of a very critical kind.

It is well known that fearful accidents occasionally happen where large grindstones are being driven at a high speed. The velocity of rotation becomes too great for the tenacity of the stone to withstand the stress; a rupture takes place, the stone flies in pieces, and huge fragments are hurled around. For each particular grindstone there is a certain special velocity depending upon its actual materials and character, at which it would inevitably fly in pieces. I have once before likened our earth to a wheel; now let me liken it to a grindstone. There is therefore a certain critical velocity of rotation for the earth at which it would be on the brink of rupture. We cannot exactly say, in our ignorance of the internal constitution of the earth, what length of day would be the shortest possible for our earth consistently with the preservation of its integrity; we may, however, assume that it will be about three or four hours, or perhaps a little less than three. The exact amount, however, is not really very material; it would be sufficient for our argument to assert that there is a certain minimum length of day for which the earth can hold together. In our retrospect, therefore, through the abyss of time our view must be bounded by that state of the earth when it is revolving in this critical period. With what happened before that we shall not at present concern ourselves. Thus we look back to a time at the beginning of the present order of things, when the day was only some three or four hours long.

Let us now look at the moon, and examine where it must have been during these past ages. As the moon is gradually getting further and further from us at present, so, looking back into past time, we find that the moon was nearer and nearer to the earth the further back our view extends ; in fact, concentrating our attention solely on essential features, we may say that the path of the moon is a sort of spiral which winds round and round the earth, gradually getting larger, though with extreme slowness. Looking back we see this spiral gradually coiling in and in, until in a retrospect of millions of years, instead of its distance from the earth being 240,000 miles, it must have been much less. There was a time when the moon was only 200,000 miles away ; there was a time many millions of years ago, when the moon was only 100,000 miles away. Nor need we here stop our argument ; we may look further and further back, and follow the moon's spiral path as it creeps in and in towards the earth, until at last it appears actually in contact with that great globe of ours, from which it is now separated by a quarter of a million of miles.

Surely the tides have thus led us to the knowledge of an astounding epoch in our earth's past history, when the earth is spinning round in a few hours, and when the moon is, practically speaking, in contact with it. Perhaps I should rather say, that the materials of our present moon were in this situation, for we would hardly be entitled to assume that the moon then possessed the same globular form in which we see it now. To form a just apprehension of the true nature of both bodies at this critical epoch, we must study their concurrent history as it is disclosed to us by a totally different line of reasoning.

Drop, then, for a moment all thought of tides, and let us bring to our aid the laws of heat, which will disclose certain facts in the ancient history of the earth-moon system perhaps as astounding as those to which the tides have conducted us. In one respect we may compare these laws of heat with the laws of the tides; they are both alike non-periodic, their effects are cumulative from age to age, and imagination can hardly even impose a limit to the magnificence of the works they can accomplish. Our argument from heat is founded

on a very simple matter. It is quite obvious that
a heated body tends to grow cold. I am not now
speaking of fires or of actual combustion whereby
heat is produced ; I am speaking merely of such
heat as would be possessed by a red-hot poker
after being taken from the fire, or by an iron casting
after the metal has been run into the mould. In
such cases as this the general law holds good,
that the heated body tends to grow cold. The
cooling may be retarded no doubt if the passage
of heat from the body is impeded. We can, for
instance, retard the cooling of a teapot by the
well-known practice of putting a cosy upon it ; but
the law remains that, slowly or quickly, the heated
body will tend to grow colder. It seems almost
puerile to insist with any emphasis on a point so
obvious as this, but yet I frequently find that
people do not readily apprehend all the gigantic
consequences that can flow from a principle so
simple. It is true that a poker cools when taken
from the fire ; we also find that a gigantic casting
weighing many tons will grow gradually cold,
though it may require days to do so. The same
principle will extend to any object, no matter how

vast it may happen to be. Were that great casting
2000 miles in diameter, or were it 8000 miles in
diameter, it will still steadily part with its heat,
though no doubt the process of cooling becomes
greatly prolonged with an increase in the dimensions of the heated body. The earth and the moon
cannot escape from the application of these simple
principles.

Let us first speak of the earth. There are
multitudes of volcanoes in action at the present
moment in various countries upon this earth. Now
whatever explanation may be given of the approximate cause of the volcanic phenomena, there
can be no doubt that they indicate the existence of heat in the interior of the earth. It may
possibly be, as some have urged, that the volcanoes
are merely vents for comparatively small masses
of subterranean molten matter; it may be, as
others more reasonably, in my opinion, believe, that
the whole interior of the earth is at the temperature of incandescence, and that the eruptions of
volcanoes and the shocks of earthquakes are merely
consequences of the gradual shrinkage of the
external crust, as it continually strives to accom-

modate itself to the lessening bulk of the fluid
interior. But whichever view we may adopt, it is
at least obvious that the earth is in part, at all
events, a heated body, and that the heat is not in
the nature of a combustion, generated and sustained
by the progress of chemical action. No doubt there
may be local phenomena of this description, but
by far the larger proportion of the earth's internal
heat seems merely the fervour of incandescence. It
is to be likened to the heat of the molten iron
which has been run into the sand, rather than to
the glowing coals in the furnace in which that iron
has been smelted.

There is one volcanic outbreak of such excep-
tional interest in these modern times that I cannot
refrain from alluding to it. Doubtless every one
has heard of that marvellous eruption of Krakatoa,
which occurred on August 26th and 27th, 1883,
and gives a unique chapter in the history of
volcanic phenomena. Not alone was the eruption
of Krakatoa alarming in its more ordinary manifestations, but it was unparalleled both in the
vehemence of the shock and in the distance to
which the effects of the great eruption were propa-

F

gated. I speak not now of the great waves of ocean
that inundated the coasts of Sumatra and Java,
and swept away thirty-six thousand people, nor do
I allude to the intense darkness which spread for
one hundred and eighty miles or more all round.
I shall just mention the three most important
phenomena, which demonstrate the energy which
still resides in the interior of our earth. Place a
terrestrial globe before you, and fix your attention
on the Straits of Sunda; think also of the great
atmospheric ocean some two or three hundred
miles deep which envelopes our earth. When a
pebble is tossed into a pond a beautiful series of
concentric ripples diverge from it; so when Krakatoa burst up in that mighty catastrophe, a series
of gigantic waves were propagated through the
air; they embraced the whole globe, converged to
the antipodes of Krakatoa, thence again diverged,
and returned to the seat of the volcano; a second
time the mighty series of atmospheric ripples
spread to the antipodes, and a second time returned.
Seven times did that series of waves course over
our globe, and leave their traces on every self-
recording barometer that our earth possesses.

Thirty-six hours were occupied in the journey of
the great undulation from Krakatoa to its antipodes. Perhaps even more striking was the extent
of our earth's surface over which the noise of the
great explosion spread. At Batavia, ninety-four
miles away, the concussions were simply deafen-
ing; at Macassar, in Celebes, two steamers were
sent out to investigate the explosions which were
heard, little thinking that they came from Krakatoa, nine hundred and sixty-nine miles away.
Alarming sounds were heard over the island of
Timor, one thousand three hundred and fifty-one
miles away from Krakatoa. Diego Garcia in the
Chogos islands is two thousand two hundred and
sixty-seven miles from Krakatoa, but the thunders
traversed even this distance, and were attributed
to some ship in distress, for which a search was
made. Most astounding of all, there is undoubted
evidence that the sound of the mighty explosion
was propagated across nearly the entire Indian
ocean, and was heard in the island of Rodriguez,
almost three thousand miles away. The immense distance over which this sound journeyed
will be appreciated by the fact, that the noise did

not reach Rodriguez until four hours after it had left Krakatoa. In fact, it would seem that if Vesuvius were to explode with the same vehemence as Krakatoa did, the thunders of the explosion might penetrate so far as to be heard in London.

There is another and more beautiful manifestation of the world-wide significance of the Krakatoa outbreak. The vast column of smoke and ashes ascended twenty miles high in the air, and commenced a series of voyages around the equatorial regions of the earth. In three days it crossed the Indian ocean, and was traversing equatorial Africa ; then came an Atlantic voyage ; and then it coursed over central America, before a Pacific voyage brought it back to its point of departure after thirteen days ; then the dust started again, and was traced around another similar circuit, while it was even tracked for a considerable time in placing the third girdle round the earth. Strange blue suns and green moons and other mysterious phenomena marked the progress of this vast volcanic cloud. At last the cloud began to lose its density, the dust spread more widely

over the tropics, became diffused through the
temperate regions, and then the whole earth was
able to participate in the glories of Krakatoa.
The marvellous sunsets in the autumn of 1883
are attributable to this cause ; and thus once again
was brought before us the fact that the earth
still contains large stores of thermal energy.

Attempts are sometimes made to explain volcanic
phenomena on the supposition that they are
entirely of a local character, and that we are not
entitled to infer the incandescent nature of the
earth's interior from the fact that volcanic out-
breaks occasionally happen. For our present purpose this point is immaterial, though I must say
it appears to me unreasonable to deny that the
interior of the earth is in a most highly heated
state. Every test we can apply shows us the
existence of internal heat. Setting aside the more
colossal phenomena of volcanic eruptions, we have
innumerable minor manifestations of its presence.
Are there not geysers and hot springs in many
parts of the earth ? and have we not all over our
globe invariable testimony confirming the statement, that the deeper we go down beneath its

surface the hotter does the temperature become?
Every miner is familiar with these facts; he knows
that the deeper are his shafts the warmer it is
down below, and the greater the necessity for pro-
viding increased ventilation to keep the temperature within a limit that shall be suitable for the
workmen. All these varied classes of phenomena
admit solely of one explanation, and that is, that
the interior of the earth contains vast stores of
incandescent heat.

We now apply to our earth the same reasoning
which we should employ on a poker taken from the
fire, or on a casting drawn from the foundry. Such
bodies will lose their heat by radiation and conduc-
tion. The earth is therefore losing its heat. No doubt
the process is an extremely slow one. The mighty
reservoirs of internal heat are covered by vast
layers of rock, which are such excellent non-con-
ductors that they offer every possible impediment
to the leakage of heat from the interior to the
surface. We coat our steam-pipes over with non-
conducting material, and this can now be done so
successfully, that it is beginning to be found
economical to transmit steam for a very long

distance through properly protected pipes. But
no non-conducting material **that** we can manufacture can be half **so** effective as the shell of rock
twenty miles or more in thickness, which secures
the heated interior **of the** earth from rapid loss
by radiation **into** space. Even were the earth's
surface solid copper or solid **silver,** both **most**
admirable conductors **of** heat, **the** cooling down
of this vast globe would **be** an extremely tardy
process ; how much more tardy must it therefore
be when such exceedingly bad conductors **as rocks**
form the envelope? How imperfectly material
of this kind will transmit heat is strikingly illustrated by the great blast iron furnaces which are
so vitally important in one of England's greatest
manufacturing industries. **A** glowing mass of coal
and iron ore and limestone **is** here urged to **vivid**
incandescence by **a** blast of air itself heated
to an intense temperature. The mighty heat thus,
generated—sufficient as it is **to** detach the iron
from its close alliance with the earthy materials
and to render the metal out as a pure stream
rushing white-hot from the vent—is sufficiently
confined by a **few** feet of brick-work, one side of

which is therefore at the temperature of molten
iron, while the other is at a temperature not much
exceeding that of the air. We may liken the brick-
work of a blast furnace to the rocky covering of
the earth ; in each case an exceedingly high temperature on one side is compatible with a very
moderate temperature on the other.

Although the drainage of heat away from the
earth's interior to its surface, and its loss there by
radiation into space, is an extremely tardy process,
yet it is incessantly going on. We have here
again to note the ability for gigantic effect which
a small but continually operating cause may have,
provided it always tends in the same direction.
The earth is incessantly losing heat ; and though
in a day, a week, or a year the loss may not be
very significant, yet when we come to deal with
periods of time that have to be reckoned by millions
of years, it may well be that the effect of a small
loss of heat per annum can, in the course of these
ages, reach unimagined dimensions. Suppose, for
instance, that the earth experienced a fall of temperature in its interior which amounted to only one-
thousandth of a degree in a year. So minute a

quantity as this is imperceptible. Even in a century, the loss of heat at this rate would be only the tenth of a degree. There would be no possible way of detecting it ; the most careful thermometer could not be relied on to tell us for a certainty that the temperature of the hot waters of Bath had declined the tenth of a degree ; and I need hardly say, that the fall of a tenth of a degree would signify nothing in the lavas of Vesuvius, nor influence the thunders of Krakatoa by one appreciable note. So far as a human life or the life of the human race is concerned, the decline of a tenth of a degree per century in the earth's internal heat is absolutely void of significance. I cannot, however, impress upon you too strongly, that the mere few thousands of years with which human history is cognizant are an inappreciable moment in comparison with those unmeasured millions of years which geology opens out to us, or with those far more majestic periods which the astronomer demands for the events he has to describe.

An annual loss of even one-thousandth of a degree will be capable of stupendous achievements when supposed to operate during epochs of geological magnitude. In fact, its effects would be so vast, that it seems hardly credible that the present loss of heat from the earth should be so great as to amount to an abatement of one-thousandth of a degree per annum, for that would mean, that in a thousand years the earth's temperature would decline by one degree, and in a million years the decline would amount to a thousand degrees. At all events, the illustration may suffice to show, that the fact that we are not able to prove by our instruments that the earth is cooling is no argument whatever against the inevitable law, that the earth, like every other heated body, must be tending towards a lower temperature.

Without pretending to any numerical accuracy, we can at all events give a qualitative if not a quantative analysis of the past history of our earth, in so far as its changes of temperature are concerned. A million years ago our earth doubtless contained appreciably more heat than it does at present. I speak not, of course, of mere solar heat—that is, of the heat which now maintains organic life ; I am only referring to the original hoard of internal heat which is gradually waning. As therefore our

retrospect extends through millions and millions
of past ages, we see our earth ever growing warmer
and warmer the further and further we look back.
There was a time when those high temperatures
which we have now found deep down in mines
were considerably nearer the surface. At present,
were it not for the sun, the heat of the earth where
we stand would hardly be appreciably above the
temperature of infinite space—perhaps some 300
degrees or more below zero. But there must have
been a time when there was sufficient internal heat
to maintain the exterior at a warm and indeed at
a very hot temperature. Nor, so far as we know,
is there any bound to our retrospect arising from
the operation or intervention of any other agent.
The further and the further we look back, the
hotter and the hotter grows the earth. Nor can we
stop until, at an antiquity so great that I do not
venture on any estimate of the date, we discover
that even at its surface this earth must have consisted of glowing hot material. We can look back
still earlier, and see the rocks—or whatever other
term we choose to apply to the then ingredients of
the earth's crust—in a white-hot and even in a

molten condition. Thus our argument has led us
to the belief that time was when this now solid
globe of ours was a ball of white-hot fluid.

On the argument which I have here used there
are just two remarks which I particularly wish to
make. Note in the first place, that our reasoning
is founded on the fact that the earth is at present,
to some extent, heated. It matters not whether
this heat be much or little; our argument would
have been equally valid had the earth only contained a single particle of its mass at a somewhat higher temperature than the temperature
of space. I am, of course, not alluding in this to
heat which can be generated by combustion. The
other point to which I refer is to remove an ob-
jection which may possibly be urged against this
line of reasoning. I have argued that because the
temperature is continually increasing as we look
backwards, that therefore a very great temperature
must once have prevailed. Without some explanation this argument is not logically complete.
There is, it is well known, the old paradox of the
geometric series ; you may add a farthing to a
halfpenny, and then a half-farthing, and then a

quarter-farthing, and then the eighth of a farthing, followed by the sixteenth, and thirty-second, and so on, halving the contribution each time. Now no matter how long you continue this process, even if you went on with it for ever, and thus made an infinite number of contributions, you would never accomplish the task of raising the original half-penny to the dignity of a penny. An ·infinite number of quantities may therefore, as this illustration shows, never succeed in attaining any considerable dimensions. Our argument, however, with regard to the increase of heat as we look back is the very opposite of this. It is the essence of a cooling body to lose heat more rapidly in proportion as its temperature is greater. Thus though the one-thousandth of a degree may be all the fall of temperature that our earth now experiences in a twelvemonth, yet in those glowing days when the surface was heated to incandescence, the loss of heat per annum must have been immensely greater than it is now. It therefore follows that the rate of gain of the earth's heat as we look back must be of quite a different character to that of the geometric series which I have just illustrated ;

for each addition to the earth's heat, as we look back from year to year, must grow greater and greater, and therefore there is here no shelter for a fallacy in the argument on which the existence of high temperature of primeval times is founded.

The reasoning that I have applied to our earth may be applied in almost similar words to the moon. It is true that we have not any knowledge of the internal nature of the moon at present, nor are we able to point to any active volcanic phenomena at present in progress there in support of the contention that the moon either has now internal heat, or did once possess it. It is, however, impossible to deny the evidence which the lunar craters afford as to the past existence of volcanic activity on our satellite. Heat, therefore, there was once in the moon; and accordingly we are enabled to conclude that, on a retrospect through illimitable periods of time, we must find the moon transformed from that cold and inert body she now seems to a glowing and incandescent mass of molten material. The earth therefore and the moon in some remote ages—not alone

anterior to the existence of life, but anterior even
to the earliest periods of which geologists have
cognizance—must have been both globes of molten
materials which have consolidated into the rocks
of the present epoch.

We must now revert to the tidal history of the
earth-moon system. Did we not show that there
was a time when the earth and the moon—or
perhaps, I should say, the ingredients of the earth
and moon—were close together, were indeed in
actual contact? We have now learned, from a
wholly different line of reasoning, that in very
early ages both bodies were highly heated. Here
as elsewhere in this theory we can make little or
no attempt to give any chronology, or to harmonize the different lines along which the course
of history has run. No one can form the slightest
idea as to what the temperature of the earth and of
the moon must have been in those primeval ages
when they were in contact. It is impossible, however, to deny that they must both have been in
a very highly heated state; and everything we
know of the matter inclines us to the belief that
the temperature of the earth-moon system must

at this critical epoch have been one of glowing incandescence and fusion. It is therefore quite possible that these bodies—the moon especially—may not then have possessed the form in which we now find them. It has been supposed, and there are some grounds for the supposition, that at this initial stage of earth-moon history the moon materials did not form a globe, but were disposed in a ring which surrounded the earth, the ring being in a condition of rapid rotation. It was at a subsequent period, according to this view, that the substances in the ring gradually drew together, and then by their mutual attractions formed a globe which ultimately consolidated down into the compact moon as we now see it. I must, however, specially draw your attention to the clearly-marked line which divides the facts which dynamics have taught us from those notions which are to be regarded as more or less conjectural. Interpreting the action of the tides by the principles of dynamics, we are assured that the moon was once—or rather the materials of the moon—in the immediate vicinity of the earth. There, however, dynamics leaves us, and unfortunately withholds its accurate illumination from the events which immediately preceded that state of things.

The theory of tidal evolution which I am describing in these lectures is mainly the work of Professor George H. Darwin of Cambridge. Much of the original parts of the theory of the tides was due to Sir William Thomson, and I have also mentioned how Professor Purser contributed an important element to the dynamical theory. It is, however, Darwin who has persistently deduced from the theory the various consequences which can be legitimately drawn from it. Darwin, for instance, pointed out that as the moon is receding from us, it must, if we only look far enough back, have been once in practical contact with the earth. It is to Darwin also that we owe many of the other parts of a fascinating theory, either in its mathematical or astronomical aspect; but I must take this opportunity of saying, that I do not propose to make Professor Darwin or any of the other mathematicians I have named responsible for all that I shall say in these lectures. I must be myself accountable for the way in which the subject is being treated, as well as for many of

the illustrations used, and some of the deductions
I have drawn from the subject.

It is almost unavoidable for us to make a surmise as to the cause by which the moon had come
into this remarkable position close to the earth at
the most critical epoch of earth-moon history.

With reference to this Professor Darwin has
offered an explanation, which seems so exceedingly
plausible that it is impossible to resist the notion
that it must be correct. I will ask you to think
of the earth not as a solid body covered largely
with ocean, but as a glowing globe of molten
material. In a globe of this kind it is possible for
great undulations to be set up. Here is a large vase
of water, and by displacing it I can cause the water
to undulate with a period which depends on the
size of the vessel; undulations can be set up in a
bucket of water, the period of these undulations
being dependent upon the dimensions of the bucket.
Similarly in a vast globe of molten material certain
undulations could be set up, and those undulations
would have a period depending upon the dimensions of this vibrating mass. We may conjecture a
mode in which such vibrations could be originated.

Imagine a thin shell of rigid material which just
encases the globe; suppose this be divided into
four quarters, like the four quarters of an orange,
and that two of these opposite quarters be rejected,
leaving two quarters on the liquid. Now suppose
that these two quarters be suddenly pressed in, and
then be as suddenly removed—they will produce
depressions, of course, on the two opposite quarters,
while the uncompressed quarters will become
protuberant. In virtue of the mutual attractions
between the different particles of the mass, an
effort will be made to restore the globular form,
but this will of course rather overshoot the mark;
and therefore a series of undulations will be originated by which two opposite quarters of the sphere
will alternately shrink in and become protuberant.
There will be a particular period to this oscillation.
For our globe it would appear to be somewhere
about an hour and a half or two hours; but there
is necessarily a good deal of uncertainty about this
point.

We have seen how in those primitive days the
earth was spinning around very rapidly; and I have
also stated that the earth might at this very

G 2

critical epoch of its history be compared with a grindstone which is being driven so rapidly that it is on the very brink of rupture. It is remarkable to note, that a cause tending to precipitate a rupture of the earth was at hand. The sun then raised tides in the earth as it does at present. When the earth revolved in a period of some four hours or thereabouts, the high tides caused by the sun succeeded each other at intervals of about two hours. When I speak of tides in this respect, of course I am not alluding to oceanic tides; these were the days long before ocean existed, at least in the liquid form. The tides I am speaking about were raised in the fluids and materials which then constituted the whole of the glowing earth; those tides rose and fell under the throb produced by the sun, just as truly as tides produced in an ordinary ocean. But now note the significant coincidence between the period of the throb produced by the sun-raised tides, and that natural period of vibration which belonged to our earth as a mass of molten material. It therefore follows, that the impulse given to the earth by the sun harmonized in time with that period in which the earth itself

was disposed to oscillate. A well-known dynamical
principle here comes into play. You see a heavy
weight hanging by a string, and in my hand I
hold a little slip of wood no heavier than a common pencil; ordinarily speaking, I might strike
that heavy weight with this slip of wood, and no
effect is produced; but if I take care to time the
little blows that I give so that they shall harmonize
with the vibrations which the weight is naturally
disposed to make, then the effect of many small
blows will be cumulative, so much so, that after a
short time the weight begins to respond to my
efforts, and now you see it has acquired a swing of
very considerable amplitude. In Professor Fitz-
gerald's address to the British Association at Bath
last autumn, he gives an account of those astounding experiments of Hertz, in which well-timed
electrical impulses broke down an air resistance,
and revealed to us ethereal vibrations which could
never have been made manifest except by the
principle we are here discussing. The ingenious
conjecture has been made, that when the earth was
thrown into tidal vibrations in those primeval days,
these slight vibrations, harmonizing as they did

with the natural period of the earth, gradually
acquired amplitude; the result being that the pulse
of each successive vibration increased at last to
such an extent that the earth separated under the
stress, and threw off a portion of those semi-fluid
materials of which it was composed. In process of
time these rejected portions contracted together,
and ultimately formed that moon we now see.
Such is the origin of the moon which the modern
theory of tidal evolution has presented to our
notice.

There are two great epochs in the evolution of
the earth-moon system—two critical epochs which
possess a unique dynamical significance; one of
these periods was early in the beginning, while the
other cannot arrive for countless ages yet to come.
I am aware that in discussing this matter I am
entering somewhat largely into mathematical principles; I must only endeavour to state the matter
as succinctly as the subject will admit.

In an earlier part of this lecture I have explained how, during all the development of the
earth-moon system, the quantity of moment of
momentum remains unaltered. The moment of

momentum of the earth's rotation added to the
moment of momentum of the moon's revolution
remains constant ; if one of these quantities increase the other must decrease, and the progress of
the evolution will have this result, that energy shall
be gradually lost in consequence of the friction
produced by the tides. The investigation is one
appropriate for mathematical formulæ, such as
those that can be found in Professor Darwin's
memoirs ; but nature has in this instance dealt
kindly with us, for she has enabled an abstruse
mathematical principle to be dealt with in a singu-
larly clear and concise manner. We want to obtain
a definite view of the alteration in the energy of
the system which shall correspond to a small
change in the velocity of the earth's rotation, the
moon of course accommodating itself so that the
moment of momentum shall be preserved unaltered. We can use for this purpose an angular
velocity which represents the excess of the earth's
rotation over the angular revolution of the moon ;
it is, in fact, the apparent angular velocity with
which the moon appears to move round the
heavens. If we represent by N the angular

velocity of the earth, and by M the angular velocity of the moon in its orbit round the earth, the quantity we desire to express is N—M; we shall call it the relative rotation. The mathematical theorem which tells us what we want can be enunciated in a concise manner as follows. *The alteration of the energy of the system may be expressed by multiplying the relative rotation by the change in the earth's angular velocity.* This result will explain many points to us in the theory, but just at present I am only going to make a single inference from it.

I must advert for a moment to the familiar conception of a maximum or a minimum. If a magnitude be increasing, that is, gradually growing greater and greater, it has obviously not attained a maximum so long as the growth is in progress. Nor if the object be actually decreasing can it be said to be at a maximum either; for then it was greater a second ago than it is now, and therefore it cannot be at a maximum at present. We may illustrate this by the familiar example of a stone thrown up into the air; at first it gradually rises, being higher at each instant than it was previously,

until a culminating point is reached, when just for
a moment the stone is poised at the summit of its
path ere it commences its return to earth again.
In this case the maximum point is obtained when
the stone, having ceased to ascend, and not having
yet commenced to descend, is momentarily at rest.

The same principles apply to the determination
of a minimum. As long as the magnitude is declining the minimum has not been reached ; it is
only when the decline has ceased, and an increase
is on the point of setting in, that the minimum
can be said to be touched.

The earth-moon system contains at any moment
a certain store of energy, and to every conceivable
condition of the earth-moon system a certain
quantity of energy is appropriate.   It is instructive
for us to study the different positions in which
the earth and the moon might lie, and to examine
the different quantities of energy which the system
will contain in each of those varied positions.   It
is however to be understood that the different
cases all presuppose the same total moment of
momentum.

Among the different cases that can be imagined,

those will be of special interest in which the total
quantity of energy in the system is a maximum
or a minimum.   We must for this purpose suppose
the system gradually to run through all conceivable changes, with the earth and moon as near as
possible, and as far as possible, and in all intermediate positions; we must also attribute to the
earth every variety in the velocity of its rotation
which is compatible with the preservation of the
moment of momentum.   Beginning then with the
earth's velocity of rotation at its lowest, we may
suppose it gradually and continually increased, and,
as we have already seen, the change in the energy
of the system is to be expressed by multiplying
the relative rotation into the change of the earth's
angular· velocity.   It follows from the principles
we have already explained, that the maximum
or minimum energy is attained at the moment
when the alteration is zero.   It therefore follows,
that the critical periods of the system will arise
when the relative rotation is zero, that is, when
the earth's rotation on its axis is performed with
a velocity equal to that with which the moon
revolves around the earth.   This is truly a singular

condition of the earth-moon system ; the moon in such a case would revolve around the earth **as** if the two bodies were bound together by rigid bonds into what was practically a single solid body. At the present moment no doubt to some extent this condition is realized, because the moon always turns the same face to the earth (a point on which we shall have something to say later on) ; but in the original condition of **the** earth-moon system, the **earth would** also constantly direct the same **face to the** moon, a condition of things which **is now** very far from being realized.

It can be shown from the mathematical nature **of** the problem that there are four states of the earth-moon system in which this condition may be realized, **and** which are also compatible with the conservation of the moment of momentum. **We can express** what this condition implies in a somewhat more simple manner. Let us understand by **the** *day* the period of **the** earth's rotation **on** its axis, whatever that may be, and let us understand by the *month* the period of revolution of the moon around the earth, whatever value it **may have ; then the** condition of maximum or minimum energy is attained when the day and the month have become equal to each other. Of the four occasions mathematically possible in which the day and the month can be equal, there are only two which at present need engage our attention—one of these occurred near the beginning of the earth and moon's history, the other remains to be approached in the immeasurably remote future. The two remaining solutions are futile, being what the mathematician would describe as imaginary.

There is a fundamental difference between the dynamical conditions in these critical epochs—in one of them the energy of the system has attained a maximum value, and in the other the energy of the system is at a minimum value. It is impossible to over-estimate the significance of these two states of the system.

I may recall the fundamental notion which every one has learned in mechanics, as to the difference between stable and unstable equilibrium. The conceivable possibility of making an egg stand on its end is a practical impossibility, because nature does not like unstable equilibrium, and a body

departs therefrom on the least disturbance ; on
the other hand, stable equilibrium is the position in
which nature tends to place everything. A log of
wood floating on a river might conceivably float
in a vertical position with its end up out of the
water, but you never could succeed in so balancing
it, because no matter how carefully you adjusted
the log, it would almost instantly turn over when
you left it free ; on the other hand, when the log
floats naturally on the water it assumes a horizontal position, to which, when momentarily displaced therefrom, it will return if permitted to
do so. We have here an illustration of the contrast between stable and unstable equilibrium.
It will be found generally that a body is in
equilibrium when its centre of gravity is at its
highest point or at its lowest point ; there is,
however, this important difference, that when the
centre of gravity is highest the equilibrium is
unstable, and when the centre of gravity is lowest
the equilibrium is stable. The potential energy
of an egg poised on its end in unstable equilibrium is greater than when it lies on its side
in stable equilibrium. In fact, energy must be

expended to raise the egg from the horizontal position to the vertical; while, on the other hand, work could conceivably be done by the egg when it passes from the vertical position to the horizontal. Speaking generally, we may say that the stable position indicates low energy, while a redundancy of that valuable agent is suggestive of instability.

We may apply similar principles to the consideration of the earth-moon system. It is true that we have here a series of dynamical phenomena, while the illustrations I have given of stable and unstable equilibrium relate only to statical problems; but we can have dynamical stability and dynamical instability, just as we can have stable and unstable equilibrium. Dynamical instability corresponds with the maximum of energy, and dynamical stability to the minimum of energy.

At that primitive epoch, when the energy of the earth-moon system was a maximum, the condition was one of dynamical instability; it was impossible that it should last. But now mark how truly critical an occurrence this must have been in the history of the earth-moon system, for have I not already explained that it is a necessary condition of the progress of tidal evolution that the energy of the system should be always declining? But here our retrospect has conducted us back to a most eventful crisis, in which the energy was a maximum, and therefore cannot have been immediately preceded by a state in which the energy was greater still; it is therefore impossible for the tidal evolution to have produced this state of things; some other influence must have been in operation at this beginning of the earth-moon system.

Thus there can hardly be a doubt that immediately preceding the critical epoch the moon originated from the earth in the way we have described. Note also that this condition, being one of maximum energy, was necessarily of dynamical instability, it could not last; the moon must adopt either of two courses—it must tumble back on the earth, or it must start outwards. Now which course was the moon to adopt? The case is analogous to that of an egg standing on its end—it will inevitably tumble one way or the other. Some infinitesimal cause will produce a tendency towards one side, and to that side accordingly the egg will fall. The earth-moon system was similarly in an unstable state, an infinitesimal cause might conceivably decide the fate of the system. We are at present in ignorance of what the determining cause might have been, but the effect it produced is perfectly clear; the moon did not again return to its mother earth, but set out on that mighty career which is in progress to-day.

Let it be noted that these critical epochs in the earth-moon history arise when and only when there is an absolute identity between the length of the month and the length of the day. It may be proper therefore that I should provide a demonstration of the fact, that the identity between these two periods must necessarily have occurred at a very early period in the evolution.

The law of Kepler, which asserts that the square of the periodic time is proportioned to the cube of the mean distance, is in its ordinary application confined to a comparison between the revolutions of the several planets about the sun. The periodic

time of each planet is connected with its average
. distance by this law ; but there is another application of Kepler's law which gives us information
of the distance and the period of the moon in
former stages of the earth-moon history. Although the actual path of the moon is of course
an ellipse, yet that ellipse is troubled, as is well
known, by many disturbing forces, and from this
cause alone the actual path of the moon is far
from being any of those simple curves with which
we are so well acquainted. Even were the earth
and the moon absolutely rigid particles, perturbations would work all sorts of small changes in
the pliant curve. The phenomena of tidal evolution
impart an additional element of complexity into
the actual shape of the moon's path. We now see
that the ellipse is not merely subject to incessant
deflections of a periodic nature, it also undergoes
a gradual contraction as we look back through
time past; but we may, with all needful accuracy
for our present purpose, think of the path of the
moon as a circle, only we must attribute to that
circle a continuous contraction of its radius the
further and the further we look back. The alteration

II

in the radius will be even so slow, that the moon will accomplish thousands of revolutions around the earth without any appreciable alteration in the average distance of the two bodies. We can therefore think of the moon as revolving at every epoch in a circle of special radius, and as accomplishing that revolution in a special time. With this understanding we can now apply Kepler's law to the several stages of the moon's past history. The periodic time of each revolution, and the mean distance at which that revolution was performed, will be always connected together by the formula of Kepler. Thus to take an instance in the very remote past. Let us suppose that the moon was at one hundred and twenty thousand miles instead of two hundred and forty thousand, that is, at half its present distance. Applying the law of Kepler, we see that the time of revolution must then have been only about ten days instead of the twenty-seven it is now. Still further, let us suppose that the moon revolves in an orbit with one-tenth of the diameter it has at present, then the cube of 10 being 1000, and the square root of 1000 being 31·6, it follows that the month must have been less than the thirty-first part of what it is at present, that is, it must have been considerably less than one of our present days. Thus you see the month is growing shorter and shorter the further we look back, the day is also growing shorter and shorter; but still I think we can show that there must have been a time when the month will have been at least as short as the day. For let us take the most extreme case in which the moon shall have made the closest possible approximation to the earth. Two globes in contact will have a distance between their centres which is equal to the sum of their radii. Take the earth as having a radius of four thousand miles, and the moon a radius of one thousand miles, the two centres must at their shortest distance be five thousand miles apart, that is, the moon must then be at the forty-eighth part of its present distance from the earth. Now the cube of 48 is 110,592, and the square root of 110,592 is nearly 333, therefore the length of the month will be one-three hundred and thirty-third part of the duration of the month at present; in other words, the moon must revolve around the earth in a period of somewhat about two hours. It seems impossible that the day can ever have been as brief as this. We have therefore proved that, in the course of its contracting duration, the moon must have overtaken the contracting day, and that therefore there must have been a time when the moon was in the vicinity of the earth, and having a day and month of equal period. Thus we have shown that the critical condition of dynamical instability must have occurred in the early period of the earth-moon history, if the agents then in operation were those which we now know. The further development of the subject must be postponed until the next lecture.

LECTURE II.

STARTING from that fitting commencement of earth-moon history which the critical epoch affords, we shall now describe the dynamical phenomena as the tidal evolution progressed. The moon and the earth initially moved as a solid body, each bending the same face towards the other; but as the moon retreated, and as tides began to be raised on the earth, the length of the day began to increase, as did also the length of the month. We know, however, that the month increased more rapidly than the day, so that a time was reached when the month was twice as long as the day; and still both periods kept on increasing, but not at equal rates, for in progress of time the month grew so much more rapidly than the day, that many days had to elapse while the moon accomplished a single revolution. It is, however, only necessary for us to note those stages of the mighty progress which correspond to special events. The first of such stages was attained when the month assumed its maximum ratio to the day. At this time, the month was about twenty-nine days, and the epoch appears to have occurred at a comparatively recent date if we use such standards of time as tidal evolution requires; though measured by historical standards, the epoch is of incalculable antiquity. I cannot impress upon you too often the enormous magnitude of the period of time which these phenomena have required for their evolution. Professor Darwin's theory affords but little information on this point, and the utmost we can do is to assign a minor limit to the period through which tidal evolution has been in progress. It is certain that the birth of the moon must have occurred at least fifty million years ago, but probably the true period is enormously greater than this. If indeed we choose to add a cipher or two to the figure just printed, I do not think there is anything which could tell us that we have over-estimated the mark. Therefore, when I speak of the epoch in which the month possessed the greatest number of

days as a recent one, it must be understood that
I am merely speaking of events in relation to the
order of tidal evolution. Viewed from this stand-
point, we can show that the epoch is a recent one
in the following manner. At present the month
consists of a little more than twenty-seven days,
but at this maximum period to which I have
referred the month was about twenty-nine days;
from that it began to decline, and the decline
cannot have proceeded very far, for even still there
are only two days less in the month than at the
time when the month had the greatest number of
days. It thus follows that the present epoch—the
human epoch, as we may call it—in the history
of the earth has fallen at a time when the progress
of tidal evolution is about half-way between the
initial and the final stage. I do not mean half-
way in the sense of actual measurement of years;
indeed, from this point it would seem that we
cannot yet be nearly half-way, for, vast as are the
periods of time that have elapsed since the moon
first took its departure from the earth, they fall far
short of that awful period of time which will inter-
vene between the present moment and the hour

when the next critical state of earth-moon history shall have been attained. In that state the day is destined once again to be equal to the month, just as was the case in the initial stage. The half-way stage will therefore in one sense be that in which the proportion of the month to the day culminates. This is the stage which we have but lately passed; and thus it is that at present we may be said to be about half-way through the progress of tidal evolution.

My narrative of the earth-moon evolution must from this point forward cease to be retrospective. Having begun at that critical moment when the month and day were first equal, we have traced the progress of events to the present hour. What we have now to say is therefore in the nature of a forecast. So far as we can tell, no agent is likely to interfere with the gradual evolution caused by the tides, which dynamical principles have disclosed to us. As the years roll on, or perhaps, I should rather say, as thousands of years and millions of years roll on, the day will continue to elongate, or the earth to rotate more slowly on its axis. But countless ages must

elapse before another critical stage of the history
shall be reached. It is needless for me to ponder
over the tedious process by which this interesting
epoch is reached. I shall rather sketch what
the actual condition of our system will be when
that moment shall have arrived. The day will
then have expanded from the present familiar
twenty-four hours up to a day more than twice,
more than five, even more than fifty times its
present duration. In round numbers, we may say
that this great day will occupy one thousand four
hundred of our ordinary hours. To realize the
critical nature of the situation then arrived at, we
must follow the corresponding evolution through
which the moon passes. From its present distance
of two hundred and forty thousand miles, the
moon will describe an ever-enlarging orbit; and
as it does so the duration of the month will also
increase, until at last a point will be reached when
the month has become more than double its
present length, and has attained the particular
value of one thousand four hundred hours. We
are specially to observe that this one - thousand
four-hundred-hour month will be exactly reached

when the day has also expanded to one thousand
four hundred hours ; and the essence of this critical
condition, which may be regarded as a significant
point of tidal evolution, is that the day and the
month have again become equal. The day and
the month were equal at the beginning, the day
and the month will be equal at the end. Yet how
wide is the difference between the beginning and
the end. The day or the month at the end is some
hundreds of times as long as the month or the day
at the beginning.

I have already fully explained how, in any stage
of the evolutionary progress in which the day and
the month became equal, the energy of the system
attained a maximum or a minimum value. At
the beginning the energy was a maximum ; at the
end the energy will be a minimum. The most
important consequences follow from this consideration. I have already shown that a condition of
maximum energy corresponded to dynamic instability. Thus we saw that the earth-moon history
could not have commenced without the intervention of some influence other than tides at the
beginning. Now let us learn what the similar

doctrine has to tell us with regard to the end.
The condition then arrived at is one of dynamical
stability; for suppose that the system were to
receive a slight alteration, by which the moon went
out a little further, and thus described a larger
orbit, and so performed more than its share of the
moment of spin. Then the earth would have to
do a little less spinning, because, under all circumstances, the total quantity of spin must be preserved unaltered. But the energy being at a
minimum, such a small displacement must of
course produce a state of things in which the
energy would be increased. Or if we conceived
the moon to come in towards the earth, the moon
would then contribute less to the total moment
of momentum. It would therefore be incumbent
on the earth to do more; and accordingly the
velocity of the earth's rotation would be augmented. But this arrangement also could only be
produced by the addition of some fresh energy
to the system, because the position from which
the system is supposed to have been disturbed
is one of minimum energy.

No disturbance of the system from this final

position is therefore conceivable, unless some
energy can be communicated to it. But this will
demonstrate the utter incompetency of the tides
to shift the system by a hair's breadth from this
position; for it is of the essence of the tides to
waste energy by friction. And the transformations
of the system which the tides have caused are
invariably characterized by a decline of energy,
the movements being otherwise arranged so that
the total moment of momentum shall be preserved
intact. Note, how far we were justified in speaking of this condition as a final one. It is final
so far as the lunar tides are concerned; and were
the system to be screened from all outer interference, this accommodation between the earth
and the moon would be eternal.

There is indeed another way of demonstrating
that a condition of the system in which the day
has assumed equality with the month must necessarily be one of dynamical equilibrium. We have
shown that the energy which the tides demand is
derived not from the mere fact that there are high
tides and low tides, but from the circumstance
that these tides do rise and fall; that in falling and

rising they do produce currents; and it is these currents which generate the friction by which the earth's velocity is slowly abated, its energy wasted, and no doubt ultimately dissipated as heat. If therefore we can make the ebbing and the flowing of the tides to cease, then our argument will disappear. Thus suppose, for the sake of illustration, that at a moment when the tides happened to be at high water in the Thames, such a change took place in the behaviour of the moon that the water always remained full in the Thames, and at every other spot on the earth remained fixed at the exact height which it possessed at this particular moment. There would be no more tidal friction, and therefore the system would cease to course through that series of changes which the existence of tidal friction necessitates.

But if the tide is always to be full in the Thames, then the moon must be always in the same position with respect to the meridian, that is, the moon must always be fixed in the heavens over London. In fact, the moon must then revolve around the earth just as fast as London does—the month must have the same length as the day. The earth must then

show the same face constantly to the moon, just as
the moon always does show the same face towards
the earth; the two globes will in fact revolve as
if they were connected with invisible bonds, which
united them into a single rigid body.

We need therefore feel no surprise at the ces-
sation of the progress of tidal evolution when the
month and the day are equal, for then the movement of moon-raised tides has ceased. No doubt
the same may be said of the state at the beginning
of the history, when the day and the month had
the brief and equal duration of a few hours. While
the equality of the two periods lasted there could
be no tides, and therefore no progress in the
direction of tidal evolution. There is, however, the
profound difference of stability and instability between the two cases; the most insignificant disturbance of the system at the initial stage was
sufficient to precipitate the revolving moon from its
condition of dynamical equilibrium, and to start
the course of tidal evolution in full vigour. If,
however, any trifling derangement should take
place in the last condition of the system, so that
the month and the day departed slightly from

equality, there would instantly be an ebbing and a
flowing of the tides ; and the friction generated by
these tides would operate to restore the equality
because this condition is one of dynamical stability.

It will thus be seen with what justice we can
look forward to the day and month each of fourteen hundred hours as a finale to the progress of
the luni-tidal evolution. Throughout the whole of
this marvellous series of changes it is always necessary to remember the one constant and invariable
element—the moment of momentum of the system
which tides cannot alter. Whatever else the friction
can have done, however fearful may have been the
loss of energy by the system, the moment of momentum which the system had at the beginning it
preserves unto the end. This it is which chiefly
gives us the numerical data on which we have to
rely for the quantitative features of tidal evolution.

We have made so many demands in the course
of these lectures on the capacity of tidal friction
to accomplish startling phenomena in the evolution
of the earth-moon system, that it is well for us
to seek for any evidence that may otherwise be
obtainable as to the capacity of tides for the

accomplishment of gigantic operations. I do not
say that there is any doubt which requires to be
dispelled by such evidence, for as to the general
outlines of the doctrine of tidal evolution which
has been here sketched out there can be no reasonable ground for mistrust; but nevertheless it is
always desirable to widen our comprehension of
any natural phenomena by observing collateral
facts. Now there is one branch of tidal action
to which I have as yet only in the most incidental
way referred. We have been speaking of the tides
in the earth which are made to ebb and flow by
the action of the moon; we have now to consider
the tides in the moon, which are there excited by
the action of the earth. For between these two
bodies there is a reciprocity of tidal-making energy
—each of them is competent to raise tides in the
other. As the moon is so small in comparison with
the earth, and as the tides on the moon are of
but little significance in the progress of tidal evolution, it has been permissible for us to omit them
from our former discussion. But it is these tides
on the moon which will afford us a striking illustration of the competency of tides for stupendous

tasks. The moon presents a monument to show what tides are able to accomplish.

I must first, however, explain a difficulty which is almost sure to suggest itself when we speak of tides on the moon. I shall be told that the moon contains no water on its surface, and how then, it will be said, can tides ebb and flow where there is no sea to be disturbed? There are two answers to this difficulty; it is no doubt true that the moon seems at present entirely devoid of water in so far as its surface is exposed to us, but it is by no means certain that the moon was always in this destitute condition. There are very large features marked on its map as "seas"; these regions are of a darker hue than the rest of the moon's surface, they are large objects often many hundreds of miles in diameter, and they form, in fact, those dark patches on the brilliant surface which are conspicuous to the unaided eye, and are represented in Fig. 3. Viewed in a telescope these so-called seas, while clearly possessing no water at the present time, are yet widely different from the general aspect of the moon's surface. It has often been supposed that great oceans once filled

I

these basins, and a plausible explanation has
even been offered as to how the waters they once

Fig. 3.—The Moon.

contained could have vanished. It has been
thought that as the mineral substances deep in

the interior of our satellite assumed the crystalline
form during the progress of cooling, the demand
for water of crystallization required for incorpor-
ation with the minerals was so great that the
oceans of the moon became entirely absorbed.
It is, however, unnecessary for our present argument
that this theory should be correct. Even if there
never was a drop of water found on our satellite,
the tides in its molten materials would be quite
sufficient for our purpose ; anything that t·des
could accomplish would be done more speedily by
vast tides of flowing lava than by merely oceanic
tides.

There can be no doubt that tides raised on the
moon by the earth would be greater than the tides
raised on the earth by the moon. The question is,
however, not a very simple one, for it depends on
the masses of both bodies as well as on their
relative dimensions In so far as the masses are
concerned, the earth being more than eighty times
as heavy as the moon, the tides would on this
account be vastly larger on the moon than on the
earth.   On the other hand, the moon's diameter
being much less than that of the earth, the effi-

ciency of a tide-producing body in its action on
the moon would be less than that of the same
body at the same distance in its action on the
earth; but the diminution of the tides from this
cause would be not so great as their increase from
the former cause, and therefore the net result
would be to exhibit much greater tides on the moon
than on the earth.

Suppose that the moon had been originally
endowed with a rapid movement of rotation
around its axis, the effect of the tides on that
rotation would tend to check its velocity just in the
same way as the tides on the earth have effected
a continual elongation of the day. Only as the
tides on the moon were so enormously great,
their capacity to check the moon's speed would
have corresponding efficacy. As the moon is
so small a body, it could only offer feeble
resistance to the unceasing action of the tide,
and therefore our satellite must succumb to
whatever the tides desired ages before our earth
would have been affected to a like extent. It
must be noticed that the influence of the tidal
friction is not directed to the total annihilation of

the rotation of the two bodies affected by it ; the velocity is only checked down until it attains such a point that the speed in which each body rotates upon its axis has become equal to that in which it revolves around the tide-producer. The practical effect of such an adjustment is to make the tide-agitated body turn a constant face towards its tormentor.

I may here note a point about which people sometimes find a little difficulty. The moon constantly turns the same face towards the earth, and therefore people are sometimes apt to think that the moon performs no rotation whatever around its own axis. But this is indeed not the case. The true inference to be drawn from the constant face of the moon is, that the velocity of rotation about its own axis is equal to that of its rotation around the earth ; in fact, the moon revolves around the earth in twenty-seven days, and its rotation about its axis is performed in twenty-seven days also. You may illustrate the movement of the moon around the earth by walking around a table in a room, keeping all the time your face turned towards the table ; in such a case as this you not only perform a motion of revolution, but you also perform a rotation in an equal period. The proof that you do rotate is to be found in the fact that during the movement your face is being directed successively to all the points of the compass. There is no more singular fact in the solar system than the constancy of the moon's face to the earth. The periods of rotation and revolution are both alike; if one of these periods exceeded the other by an amount so small as the hundredth part of a second, the moon would in the lapse of ages permit us to see that other side which is now so jealously concealed. The marvellous coincidence between these two periods would be absolutely inexplicable, unless we were able to assign it to some physical cause. It must be remembered that in this matter the moon occupies a unique position among the heavenly host. The sun revolves around on its axis in a period of twenty-five or twenty-six days—thus we see one side of the sun as frequently as we see the other. The side of the sun which is turned towards us to-day is almost entirely different from that we saw a fortnight ago. Nor is the period of the sun's rotation to be iden-

tified with any other remarkable period in our
system. If it were equal to the length of the year,
for instance, or if it were equal to the period of any
of the other planets, then it could hardly be contended that the phenomenon as presented by the
moon was unique; but the sun's period is not
simply related, or indeed related at all, to any of
the other periodic times in the system. Nor do
we find anything like the moon's constancy of
face in the behaviour of the other planets. Jupiter
turns now one face to us and then another. Nor
is his rotation related to the sun or related to any
other body, as our moon's motion is related to
us. It has indeed been thought that in the movements of the satellites of Jupiter a somewhat
similar phenomenon may be observed to that in
the motion of our own satellite. If this be so, the
causes whereby this phenomenon is produced are
doubtless identical in the two cases.

So remarkable a coincidence as that which the
moon's motion shows could not reasonably be
explained as a mere fortuitous circumstance; nor
need we hesitate to admit that a physical explanation is required when we find a most satisfactory

one ready for our acceptance, as was originally pointed out by Helmholtz.

There can be no doubt whatever that the constancy of the moon's face is the work of ancient tides, which have long since ceased to act. We have shown that if the moon's rotation had once been too rapid to permit of the same face being always directed towards us, the tides would operate as a check by which the velocity of that rotation would be abated. On the other hand, if the moon rotated so slowly that its other face would be exposed to us in the course of the revolution, the tides would then be dragged violently over its surface in the direction of its rotation ; their tendency would thus be to accelerate the speed until the angular velocity of rotation was equal to that of revolution. Thus the tides would act as a controlling agent of the utmost stringency to hurry the moon round when it was not turning fast enough, and to arrest the motion when going too fast. Peace there would be none for the moon until it yielded absolute compliance to the tyranny of the tides, and adjusted its period of rotation with exact identity to its period of revolution. Doubtless this adjust-

ment was made countless ages ago, and since that
period the tides have acted so as to preserve
the adjustment, as long as any part of the moon
was in a state sufficiently soft or fluid to respond
to tidal impression. The present state of the
moon is a monument to which we may con-
fidently appeal in support of our contention as
to the great power of the tides during the ages
which have passed ; it will serve as an illustration
of the future which is reserved for our earth in
ages yet to come, when our globe shall have also
succumbed to tidal influence.

It is owing to the smallness of the moon relatively
to the earth that the tidal process has reached a
much more advanced stage in the moon than it
has on the earth ; but the moon is incessant in its
efforts to bring the earth into the same condition
which it has itself been forced to assume. Thus
again we look forward to an epoch in the incon-
ceivably remote future when tidal thraldom shall be
supreme, and when the earth shall turn the same
face to the moon, as the moon now turns the
same face to the earth.

In the critical state of things thus looming in

the dim future, the earth and the moon will continue to perform this adjusted revolution in a period
of about fourteen hundred hours, the two bodies
being held, as it were, by invisible bands. Such
an arrangement might be eternal if there were no
intrusion of tidal influence from any other body;
but of course in our system as we actually find it
the sun produces tides as well as the moon; and
the solar tides being at present much less than
those originated by the moon, we have neglected
them in the general outlines of the theory. The
solar tides, however, must necessarily have an
increasing significance. I do not mean that they
will intrinsically increase, for there seems no
reason to apprehend any growth in their actual
amount; it is their relative importance to the
lunar tides that is the augmenting quantity. As
the final state is being approached, and as the
velocity of the earth's rotation is approximating to
the angular velocity with which the moon revolves
around it, the ebbing and the flowing of the lunar
tides must become of evanescent importance; and
this indeed for a double reason, partly on account
of the moon's greatly augmented distance, and

partly on account of the increasing length of the
lunar day, and the extremely tardy movements of
ebb and flow that the lunar tides will then have.
Thus the lunar tides, so far as their dynamical
importance is concerned, will ultimately approach
to zero, while the solar tides retain their pristine
efficiency.

We have therefore to examine the dynamical
effects of solar tides on the earth and moon in
the critical stage to which the present course of
things tends. The earth will then rotate in a period
of about fifty-seven of its present days ; and considering that the length of the day, though so
much greater than our present day, is still much
less than the year, it follows that the solar tides
must still continue so as to bring the earth's
velocity of rotation to a point even lower than
it has yet attained. In fact, if we could venture
to project our glance sufficiently far into the
future, it would seem that the earth must ultimately have its velocity checked by the sun-raised
tides, until the day itself had become equal to
the year. The dynamical considerations become,
however, too complex for us to follow them, so

that I shall be content with merely pointing out
that the influence of the solar tides will prevent the
earth and moon from eternally preserving the rela-
tions of bending the same face towards each other;
the earth's motion will, in fact, be so far checked,
that the day will become *longer* than the month.

Thus the doctrine of tidal evolution has conducted us to a prospect of a condition of things
which will some time be reached, when the moon
will have receded to a distance in which the month
shall have become about fifty-seven days, and
when the earth around which this moon revolves
shall actually require a still longer period to accomplish its rotation on its axis. Here is an odd
condition for a planet with its satellite; indeed,
until a dozen years ago it would have been pro-
nounced inconceivable that a moon should whirl
round a planet so quickly that its journey was
accomplished in less than one of the planet's own
days. Arguments might be found to show that this
was impossible, or at least unprecedented. There
is our own moon, which now takes twenty-seven
days to go round the earth; there is Jupiter, with
four moons, and the nearest of these to the

primary goes round in forty-two and a half hours.
No doubt this is a very rapid motion; but all
those matters are much more lively with Jupiter
than they are here. The giant planet himself
does not need ten hours for a single rotation,
so that you see his nearest moon still takes between two and three Jovian days to accomplish a
single revolution. The example of Saturn might
have been cited to show that the quickest revolution that any satellite could perform must still
require at least twice as long as the day in which
the planet performed its rotation. Nor could the
rotation of the planets around the sun afford the
analogy of which we are in quest. For even
Mercury, the nearest of all the planets to the sun
of which the existence is certainly known, and
therefore the most rapid in its revolution, requires
eighty-eight days to get round once; and in the
meantime the sun has had time to accomplish
between three and four rotations. Indeed, the
planets and the older satellites would seem to have
shown so great an improbability in the conclusion
towards which tidal evolution points, that they
would have contributed a serious obstacle to the
general acceptance of that theory.

But in 1877 an event took place so interesting in astronomical history, that we have to look back to the memorable discovery of Uranus in 1781 before we can find a parallel to it in importance. Mars had always been looked upon as one of the moonless planets, though grounds were not wanting for the surmise that probably moons to Mars really existed. It was under the influence of this belief that an attempt was made by Professor Asaph Hall at Washington to make a determined search, and see if Mars might not be attended by satellites large enough to be discoverable. The circumstances under which this memorable inquiry was undertaken were eminently favourable for its success. The orbit of Mars is one which possesses an exceptionally high eccentricity; it consequently happens that the oppositions during which the planet is to be observed vary very greatly in the facilities they afford for a search like that contemplated by Professor Hall. It is obviously advantageous that the planet should be situated as near as possible to the earth, and in the opposition in 1877 the distance was almost at the lowest point it is capable of attaining; but this

was not the only point in which Professor Hall
was favoured; he had the use of a telescope of
magnificent proportions and of consummate op-
tical perfection. His observatory was also placed
in Washington, so that he had the advantage of a
pure sky and of a much lower latitude than any
observatory in Great Britain is placed at. But the
most conspicuous advantage of all was the practised
skill of the astronomer himself, without which all
these other advantages would have been but of
little avail. Great success rewarded his well-
designed efforts; not alone was one satellite dis-
covered which revolved around the planet in a
period conformable with that of other similar cases,
but a second little satellite was found, which accomplished its revolution in a wholly unexpected and
unprecedented manner. The day of Mars himself,
that is, the period in which he can accomplish a
rotation around his axis, very closely approximates
to our own day, being in fact half an hour longer.
This little satellite, the inner and more rapid of
the pair, requires for a single revolution a period
of only seven hours thirty-nine minutes, that is to
say, the little body scampers more than three

times round its primary before the primary itself
has finished one of its leisurely rotations.   Here
was indeed a striking fact, a unique fact in our
system, which riveted the attention of astronomers
on this most beautiful discovery.

You will now see the bearing which the movement of the inner satellite of Mars has on the
doctrine of tidal evolution.   As a legitimate consequence of that doctrine, we came to the conclusion that our earth-moon system must ultimately
attain a condition in which the day is longer than
the month.   But this conclusion stood unsupported
by any analogous facts in the more anciently-
known truths of astronomy.   The movement of
the satellite of Mars, however, affords the precise
illustration we want; and this fact, I think, adds
an additional significance to the interest and the
beauty of Professor Hall's discovery.

It is of particular interest to investigate the
possible connection which the phenomena of tidal
evolution may have had in connection with the
geological phenomena of the earth.   We have
already pointed out the greater closeness of the
moon to us in times past.   The tides raised by the

moon on the earth must therefore have been greater in past ages than they are now, for of course the nearer the moon the bigger the tide. As soon as the earth and the moon had separated to a considerable distance we may say that the height of the tide will vary inversely as the cube of the moon's distance; it will therefore happen, that when the moon was at half its present distance from us, his tide-producing capacity was not alone twice as much or four times as much, but even eight times as much as it is at present; and a much greater rate of tidal rise and fall indicates, of course, a preponderance in every other manifestation of tidal activity. The tidal currents, for instance, must have been much greater in volume and in speed; even now there are places in which the tidal currents flow at four or more miles per hour. We can imagine, therefore, the vehemence of the tidal currents which must have flowed in those days when the moon was a much smaller distance from us. It is interesting to view these considerations in their possible bearings on geological phenomena. It is true that we have here many elements of uncertainty, but there is, how-

K

ever, a certain general outline of facts which may
be laid down, and which appears to be instructive,
with reference to the past history of our earth.

I have all through these lectures indicated a
mighty system of chronology for the earth-moon
system.   It is true that we cannot give our chronology any accurate expression in years.   The various
stages of this history are to be represented by the
successive distances between the earth and the
moon.   Each successive epoch, for instance, may
be marked by the number of thousands of miles
which separate the moon from the earth.

But we have another system of chronology derived from a wholly different system of ideas ; it too
relates to periods of vast duration, and, like our
great tidal periods, extends to times anterior to
human history, or even to the duration of human
life on this globe.   The facts of geology open up
to us a majestic chronology, the epochs of which
are familiar to us by the succession of strata
forming the crust of the earth, and by the succession of living beings whose remains these strata
have preserved.   From the present or recent age
our retrospect over geological chronology leads

us to look through a vista embracing periods of
time overwhelming in their duration, until at last
our view becomes lost, and our imagination is
baffled in the effort to comprehend the formation
of those vast stratified rocks, a dozen miles or
more in thickness, which seem to lie at the very
base of the stratified system on the earth, and in
which it would appear that the dawnings of life
on this globe may be almost discerned. We have
thus the two systems of chronology to compare—
one, the astronomical chronology measured by
the successive stages in the gradual retreat of the
moon; the other, the geological chronology
measured by the successive strata constituting
the earth's crust. Never was a more noble problem
proposed in the physical history of our earth than
that which is implied in the attempt to correlate
these two systems of chronology. What we would
especially desire to know is the moon's distance
which corresponds to each of the successive strata
on the earth. How far off, for instance, was that
moon which looked down on the coal forests in
the time of their greatest luxuriance? or what
was the apparent size of the full moon at which

the ichthyosaurus could have peeped when he turned that wonderful eye of his to the sky on a fine evening? But interesting as this great problem is, it lies, alas! outside the possibility of exact solution. Indeed we shall not make any attempt which must necessarily be futile to correlate these chronologies; all we can do is to state the one fact which is absolutely undeniable in the matter.

Let us fix our attention on that specially interesting epoch at the dawn of geological time, when those mighty Laurentian rocks were deposited of which the thickness is so astounding, and let us consider what the distance of the moon must have been at this initial epoch of the earth's history. All we know for certain is, that the moon must have been nearer, but what proportion that distance bore to the present distance is necessarily quite uncertain. Some years ago I delivered a lecture at Birmingham, entitled "A Glimpse through the Corridors of Time," and in that lecture I threw out the suggestion that the moon at this primeval epoch may have only been at a fraction of its present distance from us, and that consequently

terrific tides may in those days have ravaged the
coast. There was a good deal of discussion on
the subject, and while it was universally admitted
that the tides must have been larger in palæozoic
times than they are at present, yet there was a
considerable body of opinion to the effect that the
tides even then may have been only about twice,
or possibly not so much, greater than those tides
we have at the present. What the actual fact
may be we have no way of knowing; but it is
interesting to note that even the smallest accession
to the tides would be a valuable factor in the per-
formance of geological work.

For let me recall to your minds a few of the
fundamental phenomena of geology. Those-strati-
fied rocks with which we are now concerned have
been chiefly manufactured by deposition of sediment in the ocean. Rivers, swollen, it may be, by
floods, and turbid with a quantity of material held
in suspension, discharge their waters into the sea.
Granting time and quiet, this sediment falls to the
bottom; successive additions are made to its
thickness during centuries and thousands of years,
and thus beds are formed which in the course of

ages consolidate into actual rock. In the formation of such beds the tides will play a part. Into the estuaries at the mouths of rivers the tides hurry in and hurry out, and especially during spring tides there are currents which flow with tremendous power ; then too, as the waves batter against the coast they gradually wear away and crumble down the mightiest cliffs, and waft the sand and mud thus produced to augment that which has been brought down by the rivers. In this operation also the tides play a part of conspicuous importance, and where the ebb and flow is greatest it is obvious that an additional impetus will be given to the manufacture of stratified rocks. In fact, we may regard the waters of the globe as a mighty mill, incessantly occupied in grinding up materials for future strata. The main operating power of this mill is of course derived from the sun, for it is the sun which brings up the rains to nourish the rivers, it is the sun which raises the wind which lashes the waves against the shore. But there is an auxiliary power to keep the mill in motion, and that auxiliary power is afforded by the tides. If then we find that by any cause the efficiency

of the tides is increased we shall find that the mill
for the manufacture of strata obtains a corresponding accession to its capacity. Assuming the
estimate of Professor Darwin, that the tide may
have had twice as great a vertical range of ebb and
flow within geological times as it has at present,
we find a considerable addition to the efficiency
of the ocean in the manufacture of the ancient
stratified rocks. It must be remembered that the
extent of the area through which the tides will
submerge and lay bare the country, will often be
increased more than twofold by a twofold increase
of height. A little illustration may show what I
mean. Suppose a cone to be filled with water up
to a certain height, and that the quantity of
water in it be measured; now let the cone be
filled until the water is at double the depth; then
the surfaces of the water in the two cases will be
in the ratio of the circles, one of which has double
the diameter of the other. The areas of the two
surfaces are thus as four to one; the volumes of the
waters in the two cases will be in the proportion
of two similar solids, the ratios of their dimensions
being as two to one. Of course this means that

the water in the one case would be eight times
as much as in the other. This particular illustration will not often apply exactly to tidal phenomena, but I may mention one place that I happen
to know of, in the vicinity of Dublin, in which
the effect of the rise and fall of the tide would
be somewhat of this description. At Mala-
hide there is a wide shallow estuary cut off from
the sea by a railway embankment, and there is a
viaduct in the embankment through which a great
tidal current flows in and out alternately. At
low tide there is but little water in this estuary, but
at high tide it extends for miles inland. We may
regard this inlet with sufficient approximation to
the truth as half of a cone with a very large angle,
the railway embankment of course forming the
diameter ; hence it follows that if the tide was to
be raised to double its height, so large an area of
additional land would be submerged, and so vast an
increase of water would be necessary for the purpose, that the flow under the railway bridge would
have to be much more considerable than it is at
present. In some degree the same phenomena will
be repeated elsewhere around the coast. Simply

multiplying the height of the tide by two would often mean that the border of land between high and low water would be increased more than two-fold, and that the volume of water alternately poured on the land and drawn off it would be increased in a still larger proportion. The velocity of all tidal currents would also be greater than at present, and as the power of a current of water for transporting solid material held in suspension increases rapidly with the velocity, so we may infer that the efficiency of tidal currents as a vehicle for the transport of comminuted rocks would be greatly increased. It is thus obvious that tides with a rise and fall double in vertical height of those which we know at present would add a large increase to their efficiency as geological agents. Indeed, even were the tides only half or one-third greater than those we know now, we might reasonably expect that the manufacture of stratified rocks must have proceeded more rapidly than at present.

The question then will assume this form. We know that the tides must have been greater in Cambrian or Laurentian days than they are at present; so that they were available as a means of

assisting other agents in the stupendous operations of strata manufacture which were then conducted.   This certainly helps us to understand
how these tremendous beds of strata, a dozen
miles or more in solid thickness, were deposited.
It seems imperative that for the accomplishment
of a task so mighty, some agents more potent than
those with which we are familiar should be required.   The doctrine of tidal evolution has shown
us what those agents were.   It only leaves us un-
informed as to the degree in which their mighty
capabilities were drawn upon.

It is the property of science as it grows to find
its branches more and more interwoven, and this
seems especially true of the two greatest of all
natural sciences—geology and astronomy. With
the beginnings of our earth as a globe in the shape
in which we find it both these sciences are directly
concerned.   I have here touched upon another
branch in which they illustrate and confirm each
other.

As the theory of tidal evolution has shed such a
flood of light into the previously dark history of
our earth-moon system, it becomes of interest to

see whether the tidal phenomena may not have a
wider scope ; whether they may not, for instance,
have determined the formation of the planets by
birth from the sun, just as the moon seems to have
originated by birth from the earth.   Our first
presumption, that the cases are analogous, is not
however justified when the facts are carefully
inquired into.   A principle which I have not
hitherto discussed here assumes prominence, and
therefore we shall devote our attention to it for a
few minutes.

Let us understand what we mean by the solar
system.   There is first the sun at the centre, which
preponderates over all the other bodies so enormously, as shown in Fig. 4, in which the earth and
the sun are placed side by side for comparison.
There is then the retinue of planets, among the
smaller of which our earth takes its place, a view
of the comparative sizes of the planets being
shown in Fig. 5.

Not to embarrass ourselves with the perplexities
of a problem so complicated as our solar system is
in its entirety, we shall for the sake of clear reasoning assume an ideal system, consisting of a sun and

a large planet—in fact, such as our own system would be if we could withdraw from it all other bodies, leaving the sun and Jupiter only remaining. We shall suppose, of course, that the sun is much

Fig. 4.—Comparative sizes of Earth and Sun.

larger than the planet, in fact, it will be convenient to keep in mind the relative masses of the sun and Jupiter, the weight of the planet being less than one-thousandth part of the sun. We know, of course, that both of those bodies are rotating upon

their axes, and the one is revolving around the
other ; and for simplicity we may further suppose

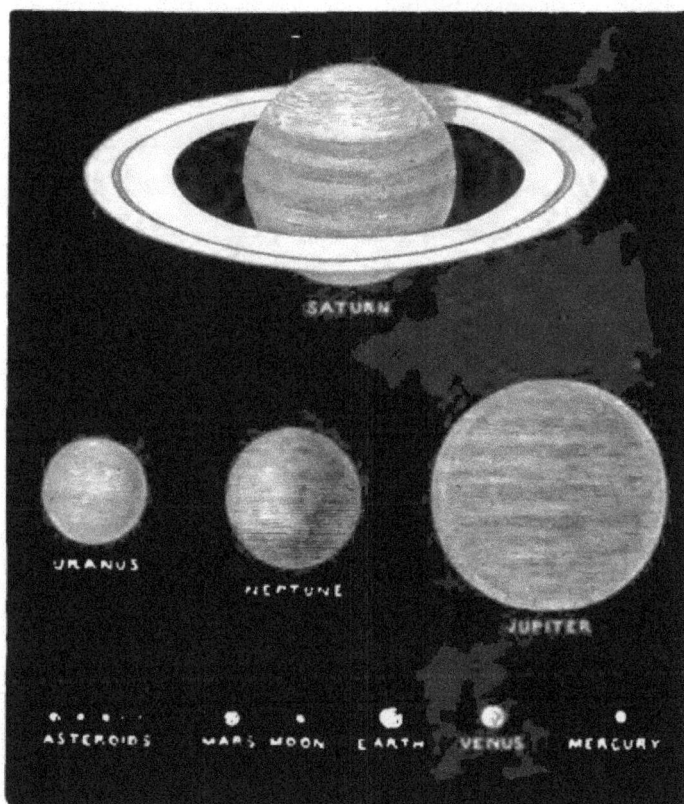

Fig. 5.—Comparative sizes of Planets.

that the axes of rotation are perpendicular to the
plane of revolution. In bodies so constituted tides

will be manifested. Jupiter will raise tides in the
sun, the sun will raise tides in Jupiter. If the
rotation of each body be performed in a less period
than that of the revolution (the case which alone
concerns us), then the tides will immediately
operate in their habitual manner as a brake for the
checking of rotation. The tides raised by the sun
on Jupiter will tend therefore to lengthen Jupiter's
day ; the tides raised on the sun by Jupiter will
tend to augment the sun's period of rotation. Both
Jupiter and the sun will therefore lose some moment
of momentum. We cannot, however, repeat too
often the dynamical truth that the total moment
of momentum must remain constant, therefore
what is lost by the rotation must be made up
in the revolution ; the orbit of Jupiter around the
sun must accordingly be swelling. So far the
reasoning appears similar to that which led to
such startling consequences in regard to the moon.

But now for the fundamental difference between
the two cases. The moon, it will be remembered,
always revolves with the same face towards the
earth. The tides have ceased to operate there, and
consequently the moon is not able to contribute

any moment of momentum, to be applied to the
enlargement of its distance from the earth; all the
moment of momentum necessary for this purpose
is of course drawn from the single supply in the
rotation of the earth on its axis.   But in the case
of the system consisting of the sun and Jupiter
the circumstances are quite different—Jupiter does
not always bend the same face to the sun; so
far, indeed, is this from being true, that Jupiter
is eminently remarkable for the rapidity of his
rotation, and for the incessantly varying aspect in
which he would be seen from the sun.   Jupiter has
therefore a store of available moment of momentum,
as has also of course the sun.   Thus in the sun
and planet system we have in the rotations two
available stores of moment of momentum on which
the tides can make draughts for application to the
enlargement of the revolution.   The proportions
in which these two available sources can be drawn
upon for contributions is not left arbitrary.   The
laws of dynamics provide the shares in which each
of the bodies is to contribute for the joint purpose
of driving them further apart.

Let us see if we cannot form an estimate by

elementary considerations as to the division of the labour. The tides raised on Jupiter by the sun will be practically proportional to the sun's mass and to the radius of Jupiter. Owing to the enormous size of the sun, the efficiency of these tides and the moment of the friction-brake they produce will be far greater on the planet than will the converse operation of the planet be on the sun. Hence it follows that the efficiency of the tides in depriving Jupiter of moment of momentum will be greatly superior to the efficiency of the tides in depriving the sun of moment of momentum. Without following the matter into any close numerical calculation, we may assert that for every one part the sun contributes to the common object, Jupiter will contribute at least a thousand parts; and this inequality appears all the more striking, not to say unjust, when it is remembered that the sun is more abundantly provided with moment of momentum than is Jupiter—the sun has, in fact, about twenty thousand times as much.

The case may be illustrated by supposing that a rich man and a poor man combine together to achieve some common purpose to which both are to contribute. The ethical notion that Dives shall contribute largely, according to his large means, and Lazarus according to his slender means, is quite antagonistic to the scale which dynamics has imposed. Dynamics declares that the rich man need only give a penny to every pound that has to be extorted from the poor man. Now this is precisely the case with regard to the sun and Jupiter, and it involves a somewhat curious consequence. As long as Jupiter possesses available moment of momentum, we may be certain that no large contribution of moment of momentum has been obtained from the sun. For, returning to our illustration, if we find that Lazarus still has something left in his pocket, we are of course assured that Dives cannot have expended much, because, as Lazarus had but little to begin with, and as Dives only puts in a penny for every pound that Lazarus spends, it is obvious that no large amount can have been devoted to the common object. Hence it follows that whatever transfer of moment of momentum has taken place in the sun-Jupiter system has been almost entirely obtained at the expense of Jupiter. Now in the solar system at present,

L

the orbital moment of momentum of Jupiter is nearly fifty thousand times as great as his present store of rotational moment of momentum. If, therefore, the departure of Jupiter from the sun had been the consequence of tidal evolution, it would follow that Jupiter must once have contained many thousands of times the moment of momentum that he has at present. This seems utterly incredible, for even were Jupiter dilated into an enormously large mass of vaporous matter, spinning round with the utmost conceivable speed, it is impossible that he should ever have possessed enough moment of momentum. We are therefore forced to the conclusion that the tides alone do not provide sufficient explanation for the retreat of Jupiter from the sun.

There is rather a subtle point in the considerations now brought forward, on which it will be necessary for us to ponder. In the illustration of Dives and Lazarus, the contributions of Lazarus of course ceased when his pockets were exhausted, but those of Dives will continue, and in the lapse of time may attain any amount within the utmost limits of Dives' resources. The essential point to

notice is, that so long as Lazarus retains anything
in *his* pocket, we know for certain that Dives has
not given much ; if Lazarus, however, has his
pocket absolutely empty, and if we do not know
how long they may have been in that condition, we
have no means of knowing how large a portion
of wealth Dives may not have actually expended.
The turning-point of the theory thus involves the
fact that Jupiter still retains available moment
of momentum in his rotation ; and this was our
sole method of proving that the sun, which in
this case was Dives, had never given much. But
our argument must have taken an entirely
different line had it so happened that Jupiter
constantly turned the same face to the sun, and
that therefore his pockets were entirely empty in
so far as available moment of momentum is concerned. It would be apparently impossible for us
to say to what extent the resources of the sun
may not have been drawn upon ; we can, however,
calculate whether in any case the sun could possibly
have supplied enough moment of momentum to
account for the recession of Jupiter. Speaking
in round numbers, the revolutional moment of

momentum of Jupiter is about thirty times as great as the rotational moment of momentum at present possessed by the sun. I do not know that there is anything impossible in the supposition that the sun might, by an augmented volume and an augmented velocity of rotation, contain many times the moment of momentum that it has at this moment. It therefore follows that if it had happened that Jupiter constantly bent the same face to the sun, there would apparently be nothing impossible in the fact that Jupiter had been born of the sun, just as the moon was born of the earth. These same considerations should also lead us to observe with still more special attention the development of the earth-moon system. Let us restate the matter of the earth and moon in the light which the argument with respect to Jupiter has given us. At present the rotational moment of momentum of the earth is about a fifth part of the revolutional moment of momentum of the moon. Owing to the fact that the moon keeps the same face to us, she has now no available moment of momentum, and all the moment of momentum required to account for her retreat has

of late come from the rotation of the earth ; but
suppose that the moon still had some liquid on
its surface which could be agitated by tides,
suppose further that it did not always bend the
same face towards us, that it therefore had some
available moment of momentum due to its rotation
on which the tides could operate, then see how
the argument would have been altered. The
gradual increase of the moon's distance could be
provided for by a transfer of moment of momentum
from two sources, due of course to the rotational
velocities of the two bodies. Here again the moon
and the earth will contribute according to that
dynamical but very iniquitous principle which
regulated the appropriations from the purses of
Dives and Lazarus. The moon must give not
according to her abundance, but in the inverse
ratio thereof—because she has little she must give
largely. Nor shall we make an erroneous estimate
if we say that nine-tenths of the whole moment
of momentum necessary for the enlargement of
the orbit would have been exacted from the moon ;
that means that the moon must once have had
about five or six times as much moment of mo-

mentum as the earth possesses at this moment.
Considering the small size of the moon, this could
only have arisen by terrific velocity of rotation,
which it is inconceivable that its materials could
ever have possessed.

This presents the demonstration of tidal evolution in a fresh light. If the moon now departed to
any considerable extent from showing the constant
face to the earth, it would seem that its retreat
could not have been caused by tides. Some other
agent for producing the present configuration would
be necessary, just as we found that some other
agent than the tides has been necessary in the case
of Jupiter.

But I must say a few words as to the attitude
of this question with regard to the entire solar
system. This system consists of the sun presiding
at the centre, and of the planets and their satellites
in revolution around their respective primaries, and
each also animated by a rotation on its axis. I
shall in so far depart from the actual configuration
of the system as to transform it into an ideal
system, whereof the masses, the dimensions, and
the velocities shall all be preserved; but that the

several planes of revolution shall be all flattened
into one plane, instead of being inclined at small
angles as they are at present; nor will it be unreasonable for us at the same time to bring into
parallelism all the axes of rotation, and to arrange
that their common directions shall be perpendicular
to the plane of their common orbits. For the
purpose of our present research this ideal system
may pass for the real system.

In its original state, whatever that state may
have been, a magnificent endowment was conferred
upon the system. Perhaps I may, without deroga-
tion from the dignity of my subject, speak of the
endowment as partly personal and partly entailed.
The system had of course different powers with regard to the disposal of the two portions; the personal
estate could be squandered. It consisted entirely of
what we call energy; and considering how frequently
we use the expression conservation of energy, it
may seem strange to say now that this portion
of the endowment has been found capable of alien-
ation, nay, further, that our system has been squan-
dering it persistently from the first moment until
now. Although the doctrine of the conservation

of energy is, we have every reason to believe, a fundamental law affecting the whole universe, yet it would be wholly inaccurate to say that any particular system such as our solar system shall invariably preserve precisely the same quantity of energy without alteration. The circumstance that heat is a form of energy indeed negatives this supposition. For our system possesses energy of all the different kinds: there is energy due to the motions both of rotation and of revolution; there is energy due to the fact that the mutually attracting bodies of our system are separated by distances of enormous magnitude; and there is also energy in the form of heat; and the laws of heat permit that this form of energy shall be radiated off into space, and thus disappear entirely, in so far as our system is concerned. On the other hand, there may no doubt be some small amount of energy accruing to our system from the other systems in space, which like ours are radiating forth energy. Any gain from this source, however, is necessarily so very small in comparison to the loss to which we have referred, that it is quite impossible that the one should balance the other. Though it is undoubtedly true that the total quantity of energy in the universe is constant, yet the share of that energy belonging to any particular system such as ours declines steadily from age to age.

I may indeed remark, that the question as to what becomes of all the radiant energy which the millions of suns in the universe are daily discharging offers a problem apparently not easy to solve ; but we need not discuss the matter at present, we are only going to trace out the vicissitudes of our own system ; and whatever other changes that system may exhibit, the fact is certain that the total quantity of energy it contains is declining.

Of the two endowments of energy and of moment of momentum originally conferred on our system the moment of momentum is the entailed estate. No matter how the bodies may move, no matter how their actions may interfere with one another, no matter how this body is pulled one way and the other body that way, the conservation of moment of momentum is not imperilled, nor, no matter what losses of heat may be experienced by radiation, could the store of moment of momentum be affected. The only conceivable way in which the

quantity of moment of momentum in the solar
system could be tampered with is by the interference of some external attracting body.   We
know, however, that the stars are all situated at
such enormous distances, that the influences they
can exert in the perturbation of the solar system
are absolutely insensible; they are beyond the
reach of the most delicate astronomical measure-
ments.   Hence we see how the endowment of
the system with moment of momentum has conferred upon that system a something which is
absolutely inalienable.

Before going any further it would be necessary
for me to explain more fully than I have hitherto
done the true nature of the method of estimating
moment of momentum. The moment of momentum
consists of two parts: there is first that due to the
revolution of the bodies around the sun; there is
secondly the rotation of these bodies on their axes.
Let us first think simply of a single planet revolving in a circular orbit around the sun.   The
momentum of that planet at any moment may
be regarded as the product of its mass and its
velocity; then the moment of momentum of the

planet in the case mentioned is found by multiplying the momentum by the radius of the path
pursued.   In a more general case, where the planet
does not revolve in a circle, but pursues an elliptic
path, the moment of momentum is to be found by
multiplying the planet's velocity and its mass into
the perpendicular from the sun on the direction in
which the planet is moving.

These rules provide the methods for estimating
all the moments of momentum, so far as the
revolutions in our system are concerned.   For the
rotations somewhat more elaborate processes are
required.   Let us think of a sphere rotating round
a fixed axis.   Every particle of that sphere will of
course describe a circle around the axis, and all
these circles will lie in parallel planes.   We may
for our present purpose regard each atom of the
body as a little planet revolving in a circular
orbit, and therefore the moment of momentum of
the entire sphere will be found by simply adding
together the moments of momentum of all the
different atoms of which the sphere is composed.
To perform this addition the use of an elaborate
mathematical method is required.   I do not pro-

pose to enter into the matter any further, except
to say that the total moment of momentum is the
product of two factors—one the angular velocity
with which the sphere is turning round, while the
other involves the sphere's mass and dimensions.

To illustrate the principles of the computation
we shall take one or two examples. Suppose that
two circles be drawn, one of which is double the
diameter of the other. Let two planets be taken
of equal mass, and one of these be put to revolve
in one circle, and the other to revolve in the
other circle, in such a way that the periods of
both revolutions shall be equal. It is required to
find the moments of momentum in the two cases.
In the larger of the two circles it is plain that the
planet must be moving twice as rapidly as in the
smaller, therefore its momentum is twice as great ;
and as the radius is also double, it follows that the
moment of momentum in the large orbit will be
four times that in the small orbit. We thus see
that the moment of momentum increases in the
proportion of the squares of the radii. If, however,
the two planets were revolving about the same sun,
one of these orbits being double the other, the

periodic times could not be equal, for Kepler's
law tells us that the square of the periodic time
is proportional to the cube of the mean distance.
Suppose, then, that the distance of the first
planet is 1, and that of the second planet is 2,
the cubes of those numbers are 1 and 8, and therefore the periodic times of the two bodies will be
as 1 to the square root of 8. We can thus see that
the velocity of the outer body must be less than
that of the inner one, for while the length of the
path is only double as large, the time taken to
describe that path is the square root of eight times
as great ; in fact, the velocity of the outer body
will be only the square root of twice that of the
inner one. As, however, its distance from the sun
is twice as great, it follows that the moment of
momentum of the outer body will be the square
root of twice that of the inner body. We may
state this result a little more generally as follows—

In comparing the moments of momentum of the
several planets which revolve around the sun, that
of each planet is proportional to the product of its
mass with the square root of its distance from
the sun.

Let us now compare two spheres together, the diameter of one sphere being double that of the other, while the times of rotation of the two are identical. It can be shown by reasoning, into which I need not now enter, that the moment of momentum of the large sphere will be thirty-two times that of the small one. In general we may state that if a sphere of homogeneous material be rotating about an axis, its moment of momentum is to be expressed by the product of its angular velocity by the fifth power of its radius.

We can now take stock, as it were, of the constituents of moments of momentum in our system. We may omit the satellites for the present, while such unsubstantial bodies as comets and such small bodies as meteors need not concern us. The present investment of the moment of momentum of our system is to be found by multiplying the mass of each planet by the square root of its distance from the sun; these products for all the several planets form the total revolutional moment of momentum. The remainder of the investment is in rotational moment of momentum, the collective amount of which is to be estimated by multiplying the angular velocity of each planet into its density, and the fifth power of its radius if the planet be regarded as homogeneous, or into such other power as may be necessary when the planet is not homogeneous. Indeed, as the denser parts of the planet necessarily lie in its interior, and have therefore neither the velocity nor the radius of the more superficial portions, it seems necessary to admit that the moments of momentum of the planets will be proportional to some lower power of the radius than the fifth. The total moment of momentum of the planets by rotation, when multiplied by a constant factor, and added to the revolutional moment of momentum, will remain absolutely constant.

It may be interesting to note the present disposition of this vast inheritance among the different bodies of our system. The biggest item of all is the moment of momentum of Jupiter, due to its revolution around the sun; in fact, in this single investment nearly sixty per cent. of the total moment of momentum of the solar system is found. The next heaviest item is the moment of momentum of Saturn's revolution, which is twenty-four per cent. Then come the similar contributions of Uranus and Neptune, which are six and eight per cent. respectively. Only one more item is worth mentioning, as far as magnitude is concerned, and that is the nearly two per cent. that the sun contains in virtue of its *rotation*. In fact, all the other moments of momentum are comparatively insignificant in this method of viewing the subject. Jupiter from his rotation has not the fifty thousandth part of his revolutional moment of momentum, while the earth's rotational share is not one ten thousandth part of that of Jupiter, and therefore is without importance in the general aspect of the system. The revolution of the earth contributes about one eight hundredth part of that of Jupiter.

These facts as here stated will suffice for us to make a forecast of the utmost the tides can effect in the future transformation of our system. We have already explained that the general tendency of tidal friction is to augment revolutional moment of momentum at the expense of rotational. The total, however, of the rotational moment of momentum of the system barely reaches two per cent. of the whole amount; this is of course almost entirely contributed by the sun, for all the planets together have not a thousandth part of the sun's rotational moment. The utmost therefore that tidal evolution can effect in the system is to distribute the two per cent. in augmenting the revolutionary moment of momentum. It does not seem that this can produce much appreciable derangement in the configuration of the system. No doubt if it were all applied to one of the smaller planets it would produce very considerable effect. Our earth, for instance, would have to be driven out to a distance many hundreds of times further than it is at present were the sun's disposable moment of momentum ultimately to be transferred to the earth alone. On the other hand, Jupiter could absorb the whole of the sun's share by quite an insignificant enlargement of its present path. It does not seem likely that the distribution that must ultimately take place can much affect the present configuration of the system.

We thus see that the tides do not appear to

M

have exercised anything like the same influence
in the affairs of our solar system generally which
they have done in that very small part of the
solar system which consists of the earth and moon.
This is, as I have endeavoured to show in these
lectures, the scene of supremely interesting tidal
phenomena; but how small it is in comparison
with the whole magnitude of our system may be
inferred from the following illustration. I represent the whole moment of momentum of our
system by £1,000,000,000, the bulk of which is
composed of the revolutional moments of momentum of the great planets, and the rotational
moment of momentum of the sun. On this scale
the rotational share which has fallen to our earth
and moon does not even rise to the dignity of
a single pound, it can only be represented by the
very modest figure of 19s. 5d. This is divided
into two parts—the earth by its rotation accounts
for 3s. 4d., leaving 16s. 1d. as the equivalent of
the revolution of the moon. The other inferior
planets have still less to show than the earth.
Venus can barely have more than 2s. 6d.; even
Mars' two satellites cannot bring his figure up

beyond the slender value of 1½*d.*; while Mercury will be amply represented by the smallest coin known at her Majesty's mint.

The same illustration will bring out the contrast between the Jovian system and our earth system. The rotational share of the former would be totally represented by a sum of nearly £12,000; of this, however, Jupiter's satellites only contribute about £89, notwithstanding that there are four of them. Thus Jupiter's satellites have not one hundredth part of the moment of momentum which the rotation of Jupiter exhibits. How wide is the contrast between this state of things and the earth-moon system, for the earth hardly contains in its rotation one-fifth of the moment of momentum that the moon has in its revolution; in fact, the moon has gradually robbed the earth, which originally possessed 19*s.* 5*d.*, and has carried it all off except 3*s.* 4*d.*

And this process is still going on, so that ultimately the earth will be left very poor, though not absolutely penniless, at least if the retention of a halfpenny can be regarded as justifying that assertion. Saturn, revolving as it does with great

M 2

rapidity, and having a very large mass, possesses about £2700, while Uranus and Neptune taken together would figure for about the same amount.

In conclusion, let us revert again to the two critical conditions of the earth-moon system. As to what happened before the first critical period, the tides tell us nothing, and every other line of reasoning very little; we can to some extent foresee what may happen after the second critical epoch is reached, at a time so remote that I do not venture even to express the number of ciphers which ought to follow the significant digit in the expression for the number of years. I mentioned, however, that at this time the sun tides will produce the effect of applying a still further brake to the rotation of the earth, so that ultimately the month will have become a shorter period than the day. It is therefore interesting for us to trace out the tidal history of a system in which the satellite revolves around the primary in less time than the primary takes to go round on its own axis—such a system, in fact, as Mars would present at this moment were the outer satellite to be abstracted. The effect of the tides on the planet raised by its satellite

would then be to accelerate its rotation; for
as the planet, so to speak, lags behind the tides,
friction would now manifest itself by the continuous endeavour to drag the primary round
faster. The gain of speed, however, thus attained
would involve the primary in performing more than
its original share of the moment of momentum;
less moment of momentum would therefore remain
to be done by the satellite, and the only way to
accomplish this would be for the satellite to come
inwards and revolve in a smaller orbit.

We might indeed have inferred this from the
considerations of energy alone, for whatever happens in the deformation of the orbit, heat is produced by the friction, and this heat is lost, and the
total energy of the system must consequently
decline. Now if it be a consequence of the tides
that the velocity of the primary is accelerated, the
energy corresponding to that velocity is also
increased. Hence the primary has more energy
than it had before; this energy must have been obtained at the expense of the satellite; the satellite
must therefore draw inwards until it has yielded
up enough of energy not alone to account for

the increased energy of the primary, but also for the absolute loss of energy by which the whole operation is characterized.

It therefore appears that in the excessively remote future the retreat of the moon will not only be checked, but that the moon may actually return to a point to be determined by the changes in the earth's rotation. It is, however, extremely difficult to follow up the study of a case where the problem of three bodies has become even more complicated than usual.

The importance of tidal evolution in our solar system has also to be viewed in connection with the celebrated nebular hypothesis of the origin of the solar system. Of course it would be understood that tidal evolution is in no sense a rival doctrine to that of the nebular theory. The nebular origin of the sun and the planets sculptured out the main features of our system; tidal evolution has merely come into play as a subsidiary agent, by which a detail here or a feature there has been chiselled into perfect form. In the nebular theory it is believed that the planets and the sun have all originated from the cooling and the contraction of a mighty heated mass of vapours. Of late years this theory, in its main outlines at all events, has strengthened **its** hold on the belief of those who try to interpret nature in the past by what we see in the present. The fact that our system at present contains some heat in other bodies as well as in the sun, and the fact that the laws of heat require continual loss by radiation, demonstrate that our system, if we look back far enough, and if the present laws have acted, must have had in part, at all events, an origin **like that** which the nebular theory would suppose.

I feel that **I have** in the progress **of** these two lectures been only able to give the merest outline of the theory of tidal evolution in its application to the earth-moon system. Indeed I have been obliged, by the nature of the subject, to omit almost entirely any reference to **a** large body of the parts of the theory. I cannot bring myself to close these lectures without just alluding to this omission, and without giving expression **to** the fact, that I feel it is impossible for me to have rendered adequate justice to the strength of the argument on which we claim that tidal evolution is the most rational mode **of** accounting **for the** present condition in

which we find the earth-moon system. Of course
it will be understood that we have never contended
that the tides offer the only conceivable theory as
to the present condition of things. The argument
lies in this wise. A certain body of facts are patent
to our observation. The tides offer an explanation as to the origin of these facts. The tides are
a *vera causa*, and in the absence of other suggested
causes, the tidal theory holds the field. But much
will depend on the volume and the significance of
the group of associated facts of which the doctrine
offers a solution. The facts that it has been in
my power to discuss within the compass of discourses like the present, only give a very meagre
and inadequate notion of the entire phenomena
connected with the moon which the tides will
explain. We have not unfrequently, for the sake
of simplicity, spoken of the moon's orbit as circular,
and we have not even alluded to the fact that
the plane of that orbit is inclined to the ecliptic.
A comprehensive theory of the moon's origin
should render an account of the eccentricity of the
moon's orbit; it must also involve the obliquity of
the ecliptic, the inclination of the moon's orbit,

and the direction of the moon's axis. I have been perforce compelled to omit the discussion of these attributes of the earth-moon system, and in doing so I have inflicted what is really an injustice on the tidal theory. For it is the chief claim of the theory of tidal evolution, as expounded by Professor Darwin, that it links together all these various features of the earth-moon system. It affords a connected explanation, not only of the fact that the moon always turns the same face to the earth, but also of the eccentricity of the moon's path around the earth, and the still more difficult points about the inclinations of the various axes and orbits of the planets. It is the consideration of these points that forms the stronghold of the doctrine of tidal evolution. For when we find that a theory depending upon influences that undoubtedly exist, and are in ceaseless action around us, can at the same time bring into connection and offer a common explanation of a number of phenomena which would otherwise have no common bond of union, it is impossible to refuse to believe that such a theory does actually correspond to nature.

The greatest of mathematicians have ever found

in astronomy problems which tax, and problems
which greatly surpass, the utmost efforts of which
they are capable. The usual way in which the
powers of the mathematician have been awakened
into action is by the effort to remove some glaring
discrepancy between an imperfect theory and the
facts of observation. The genius of a Laplace or
a Lagrange was expended, and worthily expended,
in efforts to show how one planet acted on another
planet, and produced irregularities in its orbit;
the genius of an Adams and a Leverrier was
nobly applied to explain the irregularities in
the motion of Uranus, and to discover a cause
of those irregularities in the unseen Neptune.
In all these cases, and in many others which
might be mentioned, the mathematician has
been stimulated by the laudable anxiety to clear
away some blemish from the theory of gravitation
throughout the system. The blemish was seen to
exist before its removal was suggested. In that
application of mathematics with which we have
been concerned in these lectures the call for the
mathematician has been of quite a different kind.
A certain familiar phenomenon on our sea-coasts

has invited attention. The tidal ripples murmur a secret, but not for every ear. To interpret that secret fully, the hearer must be a mathematician. Even then the interpretation can only be won after the profoundest efforts of thought and attention, but at last the language has been made intelligible. The labour has been gloriously rewarded, and an interesting chapter of our earth's history has for the first time been written.

In the progress of these lectures I have sought to interest you in those profound investigations which the modern mathematician has made in his efforts to explore the secrets of nature. He has felt that the laws of motion, as we understand them, are bounded by no considerations of space, are limited by no duration of time, and he has commenced to speculate on the logical consequences of those laws when time of indefinite. duration is assumed to be at his disposal. From the very nature of the case, observations for confirmation were impossible. Phenomena that required millions of years for their development cannot be submitted to the instruments in our observatories. But this is perhaps one of the special reasons which make such investigations of peculiar interest, and entitle us to speak of the revelations of Time and Tide as a romance of modern science.

INDEX.

THE END.

www.ingramcontent.com/pod-product-compliance
Lightning Source LLC
Chambersburg PA
CBHW030841270326
41928CB00007B/1155